Notional Syllabuses

Notional Syllabuses

A taxonomy and its relevance to foreign language curriculum development

D. A. WILKINS

Department of Linguistic Science
University of Reading

OXFORD UNIVERSITY PRESS

Oxford University Press, Walton Street, Oxford OX2 6DP

OXFORD LONDON GLASGOW NEW YORK
TORONTO MELBOURNE WELLINGTON CAPE TOWN
IBADAN NAIROBI DAR ES SALAAM LUSAKA ADDIS ABABA
DELHI BOMBAY CALCUTTA MADRAS KARACHI
KUALÁ LUMPUR SINGAPORE JAKARTA HONG KONG TOKYO

ISBN 0 19 437071 2

© Oxford University Press, 1976

First published 1976

Reprinted 1977

Printed in Great Britain by The Camelot Press Ltd, Southampton

Contents

For Roberta
and
Brigid, Alison and Jonathan

Preface

That this book is published at all is a sign of the widespread interest that the ideas it contains have already aroused. These ideas have gained some currency since they were first presented in a set of working documents of the Council of Europe and in various conference papers.[1] I was conscious at the time of the essentially interim nature of the proposals and I knew that many years of linguistic and pedagogic research would be needed before the ideas could be put forward with the authority necessary for a more substantial form of publication. For this reason I did not at the time offer the papers for general publication. If I have now changed my mind, it is because so much interest has been shown and because I am told that many people are already trying to put the ideas into practice. The original articles are not easily obtainable and in any case the central paper was not aimed at a general readership and is not entirely understandable as it stands. When I was approached by the Oxford University Press, I agreed to publication of this work in the hope that it would succeed in stimulating thought and thoughtful experimentation in the field of syllabus design. Certain modifications have been made to the framework of categories which are proposed for the construction of notional syllabuses and the justification for a notional syllabus, which makes up the first chapter, relates the issue much more explicitly to general aspects of syllabus design than was the case in the previous work. The final chapter is wholly new and attempts to explore the role of a notional syllabus in various types of language learning situations.

A work of this kind can never be the product of one person's research. I owe far more to others than I can possibly indicate. I must, in particular mention the Council of Europe which commissioned the original study on which this book is based, Jan van Ek, René Richterich

---

[1] D.A.Wilkins: 'The linguistic and situational content of the common core in a unit/credit system.' In *Systems Development in Adult Language Learning*. Strasbourg. Council of Europe. 1973.

D.A.Wilkins: 'Grammatical, situational and notional syllabuses.' In *Proceedings of the Third International Congress of Applied Linguistics*. Volume 2. A. Verdoodt (ed.). Heidelberg. Julius Groos. 1974.

D.A.Wilkins: 'Notional syllabuses and the concept of a minimum adequate grammar.' In Corder S.P. and E. Roulet (eds.): *Linguistic Insights in Applied Linguistics*. Brussels, AIMAV. Paris. Didier. 1974.

and John Trim, my colleagues on the Council of Europe committee, who encouraged me when I first put my ideas forward, and Chris Candlin and Henry Widdowson much of whose thinking I found to be similar to my own and from whom I have learned a good deal. Knowledgeable readers will be aware that some text-book writers and practising language teachers had already been working in a similar direction. I regard my own contribution as having been principally to have provided a taxonomy through which semantically oriented language teaching can be systematically planned and, secondarily, to have helped to revise our understanding of the nature of language learning and teaching in the light of these innovations.

CHAPTER ONE

Approaches to Language Syllabus Design

1.0   Introduction: synthesis and analysis

One of the major decisions that has to be taken in the teaching of foreign languages is on what basis we will select the language to which the learner will be exposed and which we will expect him to acquire. If we look at existing text-books, at existing syllabuses and at the discussions that have been conducted in journals and books devoted to the teaching of languages, we will see that a variety of approaches have been proposed or adopted. In the case of older text-books decisions appear to have been taken on a more or less subjective basis, whereas in more recent years the criteria employed have been made more and more explicit. To a considerable extent the different ways of structuring courses reflect different ways of looking at the objectives of language learning and teaching. If a close analysis of objectives has been made, the most obvious pedagogic strategy to adopt in planning to meet those objectives is to follow the components of the analysis step-by-step. Since the learning of a language is most commonly identified with acquiring mastery of its grammatical system, it is not surprising that most courses have a grammatical (or 'structural') pedagogic organisation. Of course there is enormous variety in the ways in which language may be presented in gram-matically structured teaching materials themselves, but there are also quite other ways of defining the content of language courses. There are courses based on the systematic introduction of vocabulary and others which take language situations as the starting-point. There are those that adopt a functional approach that resembles parts of the notional syllabus that is to be proposed here. The attempt has also been made to give an operational definition to the objectives of language learning and to plan courses accordingly.

While admitting that in practice these approaches are not necessarily mutually exclusive, regarding them from the linguistic point of view, I would wish to argue that they can be grouped into two conceptually distinct types of approach which could be labelled *synthetic* and *analytic*. Any actual course or syllabus could be placed somewhere on the continuum between the wholly synthetic and the wholly analytic, but the actual decision procedures that have been followed in the process of selection will show that it tends towards one pole or the other.

A synthetic language teaching strategy is one in which the different parts of language are taught separately and step-by-step so that acquisition is a process of gradual accumulation of the parts until the whole structure of the language has been built up. In planning the syllabus for such teaching the global language has been broken down probably into an inventory of grammatical structures and into a limited list of lexical items. These are ordered according to criteria which are discussed in the next section. At any one time the learner is being exposed to a deliberately limited sample of language. The language that is mastered in one unit of learning is added to that which has been acquired in the preceding units. The learner's task is to re-synthesize the language that has been broken down into a large number of smaller pieces with the aim of making his learning easier. It is only in the final stages of learning that the global language is re-established in all its structural diversity.

In analytic approaches there is no attempt at this careful linguistic control of the learning environment. Components of language are not seen as building blocks which have to be progressively accumulated. Much greater variety of linguistic structure is permitted from the beginning and the learner's task is to approximate his own linguistic behaviour more and more closely to the global language. Significant linguistic forms can be isolated from the structurally heterogeneous context in which they occur, so that learning can be focussed on important aspects of the language structure. It is this process which is referred to as analytic. In general, however, structural considerations are secondary when decisions are being taken about the way in which the language to which the learner will be exposed is to be selected and organized. The situational, notional and functional syllabuses described below (pp 15–20) are analytic in this sense, as are approaches based on operational definitions.

2.0 Synthetic approaches

The majority of language courses and syllabuses are and probably always have been constructed on synthetic lines. Language learning is a complex task. However, a complex task can usually be broken down into a series of simpler tasks. In recent years and particularly under the influence of advances in the psychology of learning the identification of the smaller learning tasks has been carried out with increasing linguistic sophistication. The tasks are identified with items derived from the description of the language. In those courses which are commonly labelled 'traditional' the control of new linguistic items introduced in any one text-book lesson or unit was not particularly strict. Whole paradigms were presented at a time and often quite distinct linguistic structures would be treated in the same lesson. In the last twenty years or so the use made by structural linguists of the technique of minimal contrast as a criterion for identifying distinct linguistic structures has encouraged text-book writers and syllabus constructors to simplify the learning task still further by reducing to a minimum the quantity of new language in any learning unit. As a result the same learning content is spread over more units and a longer period of time. However, although there is now much more explicit recognition of the criteria that are involved in this process of selecting and ordering language, the learning principle that underlies both types of text remains the same. You facilitate learning if you present the learner with pieces of language that have been pre-digested according to the categories found in a description of the language.

I should add too that matters of method and the exact form in which the new language is presented are not in question here. There are, of course, some very real differences. A new linguistic structure may be presented in the form of an explicit rule; it may be presented as a paradigm; it may be embedded in a dialogue; it may occur in a series of analogous sentences intended to promote inductive learning. None of these differences is relevant to the discussion here. If the content of teaching is in the first place a limitation and an ordering of the forms of the linguistic system, the approach is synthetic.

As methods of teaching have changed, so have the processes by which language is selected and graded. In the case of older text-books decisions appear to have been taken on a more or less subjective basis. At least there is very little discussion of the criteria that were employed. In contrast, the language teaching literature of the past thirty years or so is full of discussions of the various factors to be taken into consideration in deciding which forms of language were to be taught and in which order. This is not the place for a critical and detailed review of the literature on this topic, but a brief discussion of the criteria that have been proposed will be useful since it will be necessary to mention some of them later.

Although in most modern courses control of vocabulary and of grammatical structure go hand-in-hand, the attention of methodologists was first directed to vocabulary. This was presumably because the vocabulary that is needed for predictable day-to-day use of language was markedly different from the somewhat literary and arbitrary vocabulary that learners actually met in their predominantly reading-based courses. It was felt that ways should be found of ensuring that the vocabulary learned should be less haphazardly distributed, more in keeping with the likely needs of the learners and not so large as to constitute ᵃ severe learning burden. The aim was to see that the vocabulary content of courses consisted of, in short, the most *useful* words.

The criteria that have been used in establishing the relative useful-ness of words are *frequency*[1], *range*[2], *availability*[3], *familiarity*[4] and *coverage*[5]. The notion of *frequency* is self-evident. *Range* relates to the distribution of a lexical item over a number of different types of text. *Availability* (*disponibilité*) accounts for lexical items which may not be particularly frequent but which are readily available to the speaker when he needs them. As with *familiarity* it is measured by means of speakers' responses rather than by the statistical analysis of texts. In establishing the availability of lexical items subjects are asked to to list the words which they would find most useful in certain defined areas of interest. The degree of familiarity of an item is assessed by asking the subjects to rank words in a given list on a familiarity scale. The *coverage* of a lexical item is rated high if it expresses a range of meanings or is capable of replacing other items of more specific meaning in particular contexts.

Pedagogic considerations are not ignored in the process of selection. Some items will be promoted because they are particularly useful in

---

[1] The following works deal in some detail with vocabulary control in general and frequency in particular:

H.Bongers: *The History and Principles of Vocabulary Control.* Wocopi. Woerden. 1947.

‣ Committee on Vocabulary Selection: *Interim Report on Vocabulary Selection.* London. King. 1936.

L.K.Engels: The fallacy of word-counts. IRAL 6/3 1968

C.C.Fries and A.A.Traver: *English Word Lists.* Ann Arbor. University of Michigan. 1950.

M.A.K.Halliday, A.McIntosh and P.D.Strevens: *The Linguistic Sciences and Language Teaching.* London. Longman. 1964. Chapter 7.

A.S.Hornby: Vocabulary control – history and principles. ELT 8/1 1953.

W.R.Lee: Grading. ELT 17/3, 17/4, 18/2. 1962/63.

W.F.Mackey: *Language Teaching Analysis.* London. Longman 1965.

[2] Committee on Vocabulary Selection: *ibid.*

[3] Institut Pédagogique National: *Le Français Fondamental.* (1er degré) Paris.

R.Michéa: Mots fréquents et mots disponibles. *Les Langues Modernes.* 47.

[4] J.C.Richards: A psycholinguistic measure of vocabulary selection. IRAL 8/2 1970.

[5] W.F.Mackey and J.G.Savard: The indices of coverage: a new dimension in lexicometrics. IRAL 5/2 & 3. 1967.

I.A.Richards: *Basic English and its Uses.* London. Kegan Paul. 1943.

the classroom situation. Others will be assessed for their teachability in the light of the techniques for teaching meaning that the teacher wishes to employ. Insistence on the use of ostensive procedures, for example, will make it very difficult to teach some items in the early stages. Again, an item might be deferred where comparison with the mother-tongue suggests that it might present an exceptional degree of difficulty.

As Reibel observes, what is happening here is that we are taking the language behaviour and the language knowledge that we aim to produce in our learners, we are analysing the linguistic components of the desired performance and isolating its units. We are then teaching the units piece by piece so as to get back to the very position from which we started[6]. The process of synthesis that is required of the learner is itself based on the results of a prior analysis on the part of the course-book writer. This is true not only of the lexical but also of the grammatical content of language learning. Historically, intensive discussion of grammatical selection and grading is a more recent development, but most writers and methodologists would agree that the grammatical component is central in foreign language learning and in synthetic approaches it is the organization of the grammatical content that provides the essential structure for courses and syllabuses. Each unit of learning usually focusses on some particular aspect of grammatical structure and, whether or not this is made explicit, teachers themselves will usually identify an individual unit by means of some grammatical label.

The vocabulary that is chosen for inclusion in a general language course is only a small proportion of the total lexicon of the language. The process of selection therefore is no less important than that of ordering. With the grammar the position is rather different. The ultimate goal of a general course will be to teach virtually the whole of the grammatical system. Whereas limitation will be necessary in the case of courses of short duration or of those having as a goal some kind of restricted language competence, the problems faced in determining the grammatical content of general courses are more those of *staging* and *sequencing*[7]. By what criteria does one decide which grammatical structures will have to be taught at certain stages and how they will have been sequenced in relation to one another within each stage?

---

[6]D.A.Reibel: Language learning analysis. IRAL 7/4 1969.
[7]For a lengthier discussion of these terms see: M.A.K.Halliday, A.McIntosh and P.D.Strevens: *Op. Cit.* pp. 207–212.

The linguistic criteria that are most often cited in relation to the grammatical content of teaching are *simplicity, regularity, frequency* and *contrastive difficulty*[8]. There is no particular difficulty in understanding any of these concepts. It is suggested that more *simple* language should be taught before more complex on the not unreasonable assumption that simplicity of structure implies ease of acquisition. Judgements of simplicity are still made on a largely intuitive basis, since linguistics has not yet provided us with a means of measuring complexity which has proven psycholinguistic validity. The criterion of *regularity* requires that the most productive linguistic structures should be taught before those of low productivity. The reason why the content of the early stages of so many courses is similar is that they deal with those linguistic forms that have the greatest generalizability and whatever type of linguistic description has been used to derive the language content, the same, basic facts are likely to emerge. Some grammatical forms are so necessary to any use of the language that they can only be avoided in the early stages of a course at the cost of the greatest artificiality. The criterion of *frequency* is rarely used at all rigidly. It is more often simply a matter of deferring to a later stage the learning of forms that are evidently obscure or rarely used. A great deal has been written on the subject of *constrastive difficulty*. Most of it, however, remains at the level of description and there is very little discussion of how our understanding of particular contrastive problems influences the detail of course and syllabus design. In general it is suggested that the early stages of learning should be devoted to language forms which present the fewest contrastive difficulties.

Other criteria once again involve the interaction with pedagogic considerations. If it is intended that new language forms should be presented in a context of day-to-day language use, forms which have special *social utility* or *probability of occurrence* are likely to be

---

[8]The works by Lee, Mackey and the Institut National Pédagogique cited above also include discussion of criteria of grammatical selection and grading. Most books on methodology also contain some discussion, e.g.

J.A.Bright and G.P.McGregor: *Teaching English as a Second Language.* London. Longman. 1970.

C.C.Fries: *Teaching and Learning English as a Foreign Language.* Ann Arbor. University of Michigan. 1947.

R. Lado: *Language Teaching.* New York. McGraw-Hill. 1964.
See also:

L.Dusková and V. Urbanová: A frequency count of English tenses with application to teaching English as a foreign language, in *Prague Studies in Mathematical Linguistics.* 2. Munich. Hueber. Prague. Academia. 1967.

H.V. George: A verb-form frequency count. ELT 18/1 1963.

promoted. As with vocabulary, grammatical forms will have higher or lower priority according to their degree of *pedagogic utility,* their *appropriateness to the classroom context* and their *teachability* in the light of the methods and techniques that the teacher wishes to adopt. Most important of all is the fact that the whole of this strategy of teaching is based on the principle of working from the familiar to the unfamiliar and of using the familiar to teach the unfamiliar. The efficient teaching of one item will presuppose the prior acquisition of certain other items. The factors involved will be partly linguistic and partly pedagogic and they will result in preferred orderings of grammatical forms — what have been called *relations of recommended precedence.*[9]

One of the problems faced in selecting and grading language is that the various lexical and grammatical criteria conflict with one another as often as they complement one another and there is no way in which weightings can be given to them. A highly desirable lexical item may cause grammatical difficulties. Productive forms may nonetheless be complex. As a result, a good deal of the decision-making remains subjective. The individual teacher, writer, syllabus-constructor will, in any given instance, have to decide for himself to which criterion he will attach the greatest importance.

The syllabus that results from the application of these criteria will be a *grammatical syllabus.* The use of a grammatical syllabus can be regarded as the conventional approach to language teaching since the majority of syllabuses and published courses have as their core an ordered list of grammatical structures. The vocabulary content is secondary in importance and certainly rarely provides the basic structure of a course. The view is widely held that until the major part of the grammatical system has been learned, the vocabulary learning load should be held down to what is pedagogically necessary and to what is desirable for the sake of ensuring adequate variety in the content of learning. From this point on, the grammatical syllabus will be regarded as the archetype of a synthetic approach to syllabus design.

3.0   Reservations about synthetic approaches

In recent years a number of arguments of varying degrees of importance and validity have been put forward for questioning the adequacy of a grammatical syllabus. It is not generally denied that

---

[9] See.K.Bung: *The Specification of Objectives in a Language Learning System for Adults.* Strasbourg. Council of Europe. 1973.

what is learned through a grammatical syllabus is of value to the learner. It is rather suggested that this is not the necessary or the most effective way of designing language courses and that, in any case, language learning is not complete when the content of a grammatical syllabus has been mastered.

Reibel, in the article already referred to above, argues that the elaborate procedures of analysis leading to re-synthesis are superfluous since they aim to recreate the very language behaviour that was the starting-point of the analysis. In that case, he says, why not base language learning directly on the language corpus from which the analysis was derived? There are ways of exploiting the language found in a corpus that could lead to effective learning. However the analysis that underlies a grammatical syllabus is not often in practice based on an identifiable corpus. It is more likely to be based on existing descriptions of the language and on what, by common consent, course producers have actually included in language learning materials and syllabuses. If one shares Reibel's view, therefore, how does one choose the corpus of authentic language material on which the learning is to be based? The time available for learning is short and it does not seem reasonable to suggest that a random exposure to language will suffice. The issue of selection will still have to be faced and if one does not want to use criteria that stem from grammatical descriptions of the language, others will have to be used in their place.

One danger in basing a course on a systematic presentation of the elements of linguistic structure is that forms will tend to be taught because they are there, rather than for the value which they will have for the learner. Sometimes irregular verbs are introduced for the sake of completeness even where they are likely to be of little use to the learner. However this is a criticism of actual syllabuses not of grammatical syllabuses in principle, since the proper operation of the criteria listed above should prevent this kind of thing occurring. The danger is greatest where learners require the language for some restricted purpose. If the content is planned with general linguistic considerations in mind and with inadequate attention paid to the grammatical (and lexical) characteristics of the language performance implicit in the learners' objectives, much time may be spent in the acquisition of language that is at best marginally relevant and too little time on forms that are of particular value to this group of learners. In a word, learning will be inefficient.

One characteristic of grammatical syllabuses, a characteristic that is also found in some kinds of teaching material, is that what has to be learned is identified as a form and rarely as a set of meanings. Most syllabuses are in fact an inventory of grammatical forms. It is very rare for grammatical meanings also to be specified. The assumption seems to be that form and meaning are in a one-to-one relation, so that the meaning to be learned in association with a particular grammatical form would be self-evident. In practice, language is not like that. A single grammatical form may be semantically quite complex. The learning of grammatical meaning needs to be planned no less than the learning of grammatical forms. If this is not done, it will tend to be assumed that learning is complete when there is mastery of the formal devices or when a partial semantic interpretation can be put upon a form. In materials themselves learning of form is sometimes adequately provided for, but the learning of meaning is neglected. This kind of criticism can be met without abandoning the framework of a grammatical syllabus.

A greater difficulty and one to which there is not an obvious answer lies in the fact that the syllabus is an ordered list of structures. If the content is expressed by use of grammatical terminology, units will be identified by such labels as *the definite article, the past tense, transitive sentences, adverbs of frequency, the order of adjectives, the comparative* and so on. Alternatively the content might be expressed through examples, or, most likely of all, through both. The items that are identified in this way are only rarely syntactic structures like *transitive sentences* or *the order of adjectives* above. More often they are items which contrast paradigmatically with other items in the syllabus and which may well be morphologically distinct. By this I mean that the definite article contrasts with the indefinite article and the past tense with the present tense. Each of these is a term in a grammatical system and the total number of terms is limited. It is possible to learn all the terms of a system and the exact relationship between them. Success in learning the grammar of a foreign language is usually measured in terms of the degree of mastery over paradigmatic systems of this sort.

Although these systems are listed exhaustively in a syllabus, the syntactic structures in which they occur in the language are not. Of course the fundamental facts of syntax are almost inevitably taught, but there remains a good deal that is not. Let us take an example. In the unit labelled *comparative* the learner will learn such facts as that *older* is in contrast with *old* and *oldest*. He will learn that this is a typical comparative formation and that certain other adjectives form their comparatives differently. He will also learn that a comparative adjective co-occurs with *than* and he will probably practise the comparative through syntactic structures like *John is older than Peter*. What the syllabus or the course will never do, either at this point or at a later stage, is make it clear that the comparative occurs in sentences like *the ruins were older to a considerable degree than had originally been thought* or *older than the discovery of electricity was the invention of the steam-engine.* A multiplicity of other comparative sentences are also possible, all syntactically distinct from one another. The fact is, therefore, that the inventories found in grammatical syllabuses give insufficient attention to syntax.

There is a good reason why this should be so. The actual number of structures (sentences) that are possible in any language is infinite. This is because, as linguists have recently once again emphasized, a finite set of grammatical rules is capable of producing an infinity of sentences. Any syllabus which is an itemized list of points or structures to be learned is inevitably incomplete. It is impossible therefore, for a grammatical syllabus to cover the grammatical facts exhaustively. On the other hand they could (and should) be modified to take greater account of the importance of the acquisition of syntax. It would not be difficult even within a grammatical syllabus to show that sentence structures can be extremely varied, so that the learner is not encouraged to believe that what he is being taught constitutes *the* structures of the language.

One of the major reasons for questioning the adequacy of grammatical syllabuses lies in the fact that even when we have described the grammatical (and lexical) meaning of a sentence we have not accounted for the way in which it is used as an utterance. It is this apparent paradox that has led philosophers to try to define meaning as use. The fact is that sentences are not confined in use to the functions suggested by the grammatical labels that we give to them, nor does one use of language require the selection of one particular grammatical form. In an interesting discussion of the pedagogic significance of the discrepancy between what is signified grammatically and what is actually communicated Widdowson makes the following observation:[10]

> One might imagine, for example, that the imperative mood is an unequivocal indicator of the act of commanding. But consider these instances of the imperative: 'Bake the pie in a slow oven', 'Come for dinner tomorrow', 'Take up his offer', 'Forgive us our trespasses'. An instruction, an invitation, advice and prayer are all different acts, yet the imperative serves them all; — and need serve none of them: 'You must bake the pie in a slow oven', 'Why don't you come to dinner tomorrow?' 'I should take up his offer', 'We pray for forgiveness of our trespasses'. But one might suppose, neverthe-

---

[10] H.G.Widdowson: The teaching of rhetoric to students of science and technology. In *Science and Technology in a Second Language.* London. Centre for Information on Language Teaching and Research. 1971. pp. 38–39.

less, that though there are several different kinds of act that can be performed by the imperative, when an order is to be given, it is always the imperative which is used. But this, of course, is not the case either. Just as one linguistic form may fulfil a variety of rhetorical functions, so one rhetorical function may be fulfilled by a variety of linguistic forms.

Widdowson then quotes a number of examples from Labov of the different way in which a teacher may phrase a command.[11]

This should be done again.
You'll have to do this again.
You can do better than this.
It's my job to get you to do better than this.

Given the teacher's relationship to his pupils, these will all be intended as commands and, indeed, will be interpreted as such, although, of course, these sentences are not synonymous.

The most significant thing about this example is that the teacher will normally be understood as he intends to be understood. If this was not so, communication could scarcely take place. We are able to convey grammatical meaning in any situation where speaker and hearer are familiar with the grammatical system. The hearer knows the grammatical rules that the speaker is using. Since those things that are not conveyed by the grammar are also understood, they too must be governed by 'rules' which are known to both speaker and hearer. People who speak the same language share not so much a *grammatical* competence as a *communicative* competence.

Looked at in foreign language learning terms, this means that the learner has to learn rules of communication as well as rules of grammar. The conventions that relate the linguistic form of an utterance to its actual communicative effect are not universal. What is permissible in the use of one language may not be permissible in another. Since there will be similarities and differences between languages, the learning of the communicative conventions no less than the learning of the grammatical conventions has to be planned for. A grammatical syllabus, however, provides for the acquisition of a grammatical competence and embodies the assumption either that grammatical function and communicative function are the same thing, or that the learner himself can readily acquire knowledge of the communicative aspects of language during or after his acquisition of the grammatical system. The aim of the present study is to find a better way of taking account of the communicative aspects of language than is possible within the framework of a grammatical syllabus.

---

[11] W.Labov: *The Study of Non-standard English.* National Council of Teachers of English. (U.S.A.). 1969. pp. 54–56.

For learners, probably the most striking way in which the knowledge of language developed through a grammatical syllabus fails to
measure up to their communicational needs is in its lack of situational
relevance. They may have learned through oral, active methods and,
indeed, have a considerable practical command of grammatical
structures, but the language that they rehearse in the classroom will be
inadequately related to what is needed in the situations in which they
may actually want to use the language. Even the relatively uninformed
learner is aware that there are ways of using language that are appropriate to the situation in which and for which it is required. What one
may want to say in one situation differs from what is needed in
another. Some specialised uses of language are quite distinctive and
there is enough variety in language for one to be cautious about regarding language as a monolithic whole. The language that occurs in
any one situation can be regarded as a sub-variety of the whole in the
particular way in which it exploits the grammatical core of the
language. The grammatical syllabus focusses learning on the core and
not on the distribution of that core in particular uses. As a result,
even the learner who knows the core may not be able to communicate
adequately when he finds himself in a situation requiring language.

I should add that there is language teaching, based on a grammatical syllabus, which is sometimes called *situational.* The label is most
commonly applied to a method of teaching in which language is
always taught in association with some physical characteristic of the
classroom. Objects, pictures and activities are used to illustrate and
give meaning to grammatical and lexical forms. Tenses, for example,
are often presented in association with physical activities on the part
of teacher or pupils. It is clear, however, that the situation referred to
here is a pedagogic, classroom situation, not a situation of natural
language use. It cannot, therefore, meet situational language needs,
however effective it might be as a pedagogic device. A grammatical
syllabus can also be 'situationalized' by presenting language in the
form of dialogues. The dialogues are written to illustrate a grammatical
point and apart from the use of situationally restricted formulae, they
rarely resemble natural language use, nor do they enlighten the learner's
understanding of the appropriateness of form to context and purpose.
An interesting point about virtually all modern courses derived from a
grammatical syllabus is that the intensive practice materials involve
the repeated production of sentences having like structures. Such
sentences are not related to one another thematically as would be the
case in natural language use. Equally, in natural language interaction
sentences of identical structure scarcely ever co-occur. Neither of these
approaches represent any radical revision of the grammatical syllabus

to take account of situational needs.

The contrast between language as it is experienced in the classroom and language as it is known to be used in society often makes it difficult for the learner to appreciate the value of what he is learning. The motivation of learners is hard to sustain when success is measured in terms of the proportion of the grammatical system known. Although some learners are able to see that an investment in learning effort now should produce practical benefits in the future, many are looking for a much more immediate return for the effort expended. Their motivation will be less likely to fade if they are continually aware that this is not an unapplied, and from their point of view perhaps unapplicable system, but a genuine means of communication. The argument is the stronger if the learners are already in a situation where they can or need to use the language they are learning. On grounds of motivation, therefore, as well as on linguistic grounds, there are reasons for looking for an alternative to the grammatical syllabus as a strategy for structuring the learner's experience of language.

4.0   Analytic approaches

The prior analysis of the total language system into a set of discrete pieces of language that is a necessary precondition for the adoption of a synthetic approach is largely superfluous in an analytic approach. As we shall see, this is not to say that we make no use of the structural facts of language in making decisions, merely that they are not the starting-point. Analytic approaches are behavioural (though not behaviour*ist*). They are organized in terms of the purposes for which people are learning language and the kinds of language performance that are necessary to meet those purposes. The problem of putting an analytic approach into practice is largely one of finding a way to express what it is that people do with language, so that the unavoidable process of limitation or selection can take place. The units in any language teaching material based on an analytic approach are not primarily labelled in grammatical terms. They are identified according to whatever behavioural metalanguage we have eventually decided upon. Of course, since it is language behaviour we are concerned with, it is possible, indeed desirable, that the linguistic content of any unit should also be stated, but it is a content that is derived from the initial behavioural analysis. It cannot be established independently of it.

Actual language behaviour is structurally very varied and since the organization of teaching in analytic approaches is in terms of types of actual language behaviour, structural diversity in any analytic syllabus or teaching materials is inevitable. In the actual teaching process pieces of this heterogeneous structural content will be extracted and isolated so that learning can be focussed upon them. The need for the learner to benefit from significant linguistic generalizations cannot be ignored, but the units of language treated in this way will not necessarily be minimally distinct from one another as is usually the case in synthetic approaches. Whether or not the aspects of language structure involved are brought explicity to the learner's attention is a methodological matter and does not concern us directly here. However, since we are inviting the learner, directly or indirectly, to recognize the linguistic components of the language behaviour he is acquiring, we are in effect basing our approach on the learner's analytic capacities. This approach is therefore in contrast with those approaches that rely more upon his capacity to synthesize.

4.1   Operational definitions

An operational definition is a way of stating terminal or intermediate objectives rather than a way of constructing actual teaching sequences. The statement of objectives would not normally include a specification of linguistic structures, that is to say, there would be no inventory of words or structures such as we have seen above. As the components of the language behaviour are not specified, the learner's task cannot be one of re-synthesis. Operational definitions are, therefore, here categorized as analytical. The potential of operational definitions in language teaching is largely unexplored, so that there is only brief discussion of the issue here.

As the name suggests, the essence of an operational definition is that it defines the operations that the individual is capable of performing. In the case of language behaviour the operations are language operations. The operations themselves must be identified in such a way as to be measurable in strictly quantitative terms. The quantities themselves should reflect identifiable aspects of behaviour. The approach is perhaps best understood through some examples.

We could set as objectives for a science student studying through the medium of a foreign language that he should be able to read student text-books in his field of specialization at a rate of x words per minute (w.p.m.) and with y degree of comprehension (as measured by some standard form of comprehension measurement). An intermediate objective for the same student might be that he could read the same type of text with the same degree of comprehension but at a rate of $\frac{x}{2}$ w.p.m. Alternatively the rate could be kept stable but the degree of comprehension varied. Objectives for a secretary could be that she should be able to take foreign language dictation given at x w.p.m. with y degree of accuracy. In setting intermediate goals, x and y could be varied, although, presumably, the ultimate value of y would have to be 100%. This would also apply to an interpreter whose capacity in simultaneous interpreting can be measured in terms of rate and accuracy.

These are two interesting things about these examples. In all cases the form of the linguistic input to the learner is held constant. There is no attempt to define such notions as *elementary*, *intermediate* and *advanced* in terms of the degree of complexity of the language structure, as would be the case in a synthetic approach. The language is the language of the terminal behaviour and levels of proficiency are assessed in terms of the degree of capacity to perform the terminal behaviour itself. Levels of proficiency indicated in these terms are more easily relatable to actual language performance than statements of numbers of linguistic structures or lexical items known.

The second point is that in each of these examples the language performance takes the form of a response to a clearly identifiable external linguistic stimulus. It is unlikely that other kinds of language performance could be identified and measured in such simple terms. Much of our production of language is not relatable to external stimuli in this way. It is true that the situational and semantic dimensions that are discussed below are capable of handling productive aspects of language and that, at the same time, they can be thought of as contributing to operational definitions. In that case, however, it is clear that measurement of language proficiency is not going to be quite as straightforward as the above examples suggest. The full operationalization of language teaching objectives still seems to be something for the future.

4.2   Situational syllabuses

I have suggested that the framework for most foreign language teaching is provided by a grammatical syllabus and that dissatisfaction with this shows itself most readily in concern that the language acquired in this way is not adequate for situational needs. It is hardly surprising, therefore, that the most commonly proposed alternative is to take situational needs as the starting-point and thereby to construct a *situational syllabus* to replace the grammatical syllabus. It is the only other kind of syllabus that is at all widely used as a basis for the construction of teaching materials.

The argument for the situational syllabus is fairly straightforward. Although languages are usually described as general systems, language is always used in a social context and cannot be fully understood without reference to that context. Our choice of linguistic forms may be restricted according to certain features of the social situation and, in any case, we need the language so that we can use it in the situations that we encounter. Therefore, rather than orientate learning to the subject and its content, we should take account of the learner and his needs. We should predict the situations in which the learner is likely to need the language and then teach the language that is necessary to perform linguistically in those situations. It will be a more efficient process because it will include only what is relevant to the learner. It will be more motivating because it is learner- rather than subject-centred. The distinction between language for learning and language for use will disappear. Units in the syllabus will have situational instead of grammatical labels.

In order to carry out the behavioural analysis that underlies the situational syllabus, we must have a set of parameters for describing the significant features of situations. These features include the physical context in which the language event occurs, the channel (spoken or written) of communication, whether the language activity is productive or receptive, the number and the character of the participants, the relationships between them and the field of activity within which the language event is taking place. Obviously, different syllabuses will result for different types of learner. The exact contents of a syllabus will be the result of a careful behavioural prediction and will consist of an inventory of language situations and a description of the linguistic content of each of these situations.

Situational courses do exist. They consist of learning units with labels like 'At the post office', 'Buying a theatre ticket', 'Asking the way' and so on. In all probability they are successful in what they set out to do, but there are reasons for doubting whether they can be taken as a model for the general organization of language teaching. The difficulty centres on just what is meant by 'situation'. With examples like the ones above there is no great difficulty. They are situations with fairly evident, objectively describable physical characteristics. The language interactions that are taking place are closely related to the situation itself. There will be grammatical and lexical forms that have a high probability of occurrence in these kinds of language event.

However it would be naive to think that the speaker is somehow
linguistically at the mercy of the physical situation in which he finds
himself. What the individual says is what he has chosen to say. It is a
matter of his intentions and purposes. The fact that there are some
situations in which certain intentions are regularly expressed, certain
linguistic transactions regularly carried out, does not mean that this is
typical of our language use. Even in the restricted physical situations
that have been mentioned so far language does not have to be
related to the situation. I may have gone into the post office, not to
buy stamps, but to complain about the non-arrival of a parcel, to
change some money so that I can make a telephone call or to ask a
friend of mine who works behind the counter whether he wants to
come to a football match on Saturday afternoon. Making complaints
is not (or should not be!) what one typically goes to a post office for.
The making of requests, the seeking of information, the expression of
agreement and disagreement can take place in almost any situation.
There are probably no situations where we typically express possibility, probability, certainty, doubt or conviction and yet the need
to do so is demonstrated by the frequency with which they are
expressed in our speech.

One way in which this problem might be overcome is by extending
the notion of situation to include uses of language like those just
mentioned which are the product of internal processes and not of the
influence of situational features. Once we do this, however, we move
into the realms of the unpredictable. The content of an utterance is
determined by the state of mind of the speaker. That in turn is the
product of his life's experience. We could predict his language
behaviour only if we had complete knowledge of the universe. By
broadening the concept of situation in this way we have rendered it
virtually inoperable since we are no longer able to describe the
features of a situation in objective terms. At the same time we have
lost the benefit of the insight into language that is provided by our
awareness that relationships between language and situation do exist.

It seems best, therefore, to retain the term *situation* for the sum of
the observable and independently describable features of the context
in which a language event occurs. Language use is then seen as a
continuum. At one end of the scale the form and content of utterances
is fairly predictable from a description of the situational context. At
the other end the situational context of utterance is almost wholly
irrelevant and prediction would be possible only if one knew what, in
practice, one cannot know — the learned and inherited characteristics
of the participants.

Examples of language use under the control of observable stimuli

are, if anything, atypical. A situational syllabus will be valuable inso-
far as a learner's need is to be able to handle language situations of this
sort. The limited aims of a tourist, a waiter or a telephone switchboard
operator might be provided for adequately in this way. However, they
would, by definition, be unprepared for anything 'out of the ordinary'.
If we were to attempt to use a situational syllabus for any learner
whose needs could not be identified in these situational terms, including the general language learner, we would fail to provide him with the
means to handle significant language needs. Useful as a situational
syllabus may be in certain circumstances, therefore, it does not offer a
general solution to problems of syllabus design.[12]

4.3   Notional syllabuses

The discussion so far has suggested that there are limits to what can
be achieved through grammatical and situational syllabuses. The
grammatical syllabus seeks to teach the language by taking the learner
progressively through the forms of the target language. The situational
syllabus does so by recreating the situations in which native speakers
use the language. While in neither case would it be denied that
languages are learned for the purposes of communication, both leave
the learner short of adequate communicative capacity. We have now,
in effect, dealt with the existing situation in syllabus design and in
doing so have provided a context against which the proposals for a
notional syllabus, which are the major concern of the present book,
can best be understood and judged.

The notional syllabus is in contrast with the other two because it
takes the desired communicative capacity as the starting-point. In
drawing up a notional syllabus, instead of asking how speakers of the
language express themselves or when and where they use the language,
we ask what it is they communicate through language. We are then
able to organize language teaching in terms of the content rather than
the form of the language. For this reason the resulting syllabus is
called a *notional syllabus.*[13]

[12] I should, perhaps, point out that the conceptual distinction between, say,
a grammatical and a situational syllabus need not always be so clearly drawn in
practice. A grammatical syllabus could be situationalized to the extent that a
situational context (e.g. in the form of a dialogue) could be created to illustrate
the grammatical structure being presented. A situational syllabus may similarly
be grammaticalized by the deliberate exclusion or inclusion of grammatical
structures in otherwise 'natural' materials. Neither of these processes can obscure
the fundamental contrast in the underlying strategies.
[13] The term *notional* is borrowed from linguistics where grammars based on
semantic criteria are commonly called *notional grammars* (cf. *formal grammars*
where the criteria used in analysis are *formal*).

The advantage of the notional syllabus is that it takes the communicative facts of language into account from the beginning without losing sight of grammatical and situational factors. It is potentially superior to the grammatical syllabus because it will produce a communicative competence and because its evident concern with the use of language will sustain the motivation of the learners. It is superior the the situational syllabus because it can ensure that the most important grammatical forms are included and because it can cover all kinds of language functions, not only those that typically occur in certain situations.

The process of deciding what to teach is based on consideration of what the learners should most usefully be able to communicate in the foreign language. When this is established, we can decide what are the most appropriate forms for each type of communication. The labelling for the learning units is now primarily semantic, although there is no reason why the structural realization should not also be indicated. A general language course will concern itself with those concepts and functions[14] that are likely to be of widest value. In the same way, in the provision of a course for a more specialized language learner, the limitation is on the types of content that he needs to express and not on the number of structures he needs to know or the situations in which he will find himself. In short, the linguistic content is planned according to the semantic demands of the learner.

Although, as we shall see in the final chapter, the criteria that are used in establishing a grammatical syllabus need not be wholly irrelevant in the creation of a notional syllabus, there is no reason to expect that what we identify as being semantically necessary to the learner will coincide with what is grammatically the most simple, the most regular or the easiest to learn. To put it another way, the forms that are needed to express the semantic needs will be extremely varied. Even if one could identify a 'simple' need, it is unlikely that there would be a 'simple' form that met it. The learning material derived from a notional syllabus will, therefore, almost inevitably be linguistically heterogeneous. Although we will probably choose to isolate particular forms from this rich linguistic enviornment to ensure adequate learning of the grammatical system, there will be no ordered exposure to the grammar of the language. A notional syllabus is, therefore, to be classified as an example of an analytic approach to language teaching.

We can now see the position of the notional syllabus in relation to other forms of syllabus design. We have also seen what considerations

---

[14] The exact sense in which these terms are used here is explained on pp 23-24

motivate the proposal that we should approach syllabus construction from semantics. The remainder of this study is devoted to a more detailed examination of the concept of a notional syllabus, but, first, there is one major difficulty that has to be overcome. Whereas in the case of the grammatical syllabus a framework is readily available in the form of one of the many descriptions of the language and in the case of the situational syllabus much progress has been made in recent years in identifying the relevant situational features, when it comes to attempting to produce a notional syllabus, there is no available semantic (notional) framework in terms of which it can be prepared. The next chapter, which constitutes the major part of this study, is devoted to the exposition and exemplification of a framework which could be used in the setting-up of a notional syllabus. In the final chapter there is discussion of the way in which the framework might be used in producing a notional syllabus and of the language teaching situations in which a notional syllabus might most valuably be adopted. There is also consideration of some of the implications of a notional approach for other aspects of language teaching.

CHAPTER TWO

Categories for a Notional Syllabus

1.0   Introduction: the components of a notional syllabus

There are many dimensions to the meaning of sentences and
utterances. The combination of grammar, lexis, stylistics, linguistic
and non-linguistic context and, in speech, intonation ensures that any
two sentences only very rarely have exactly the same meaning. A
system capable of handling all the content of utterances would have to
be able to represent all the semantic information found in a grammar,
a dictionary and a thesaurus. Obviously such a system would not be
very manageable for practical purposes and indeed only in exceptional
circumstances can it be the aim of language teaching to predict and
prepare for the individual utterances that the learner will want to
produce. It is therefore with general aspects of meaning and use that
the categories presented here are concerned, though they are not the
less significant for being general in character. This also explains why
no attempt is made within this framework to account for the lexical
content of learning. This is probably better approached in terms of
subject-matter and situation. At the same time, lexical aspects cannot
be entirely excluded since grammatical and lexical devices often
interact significantly.

For the purposes of this study we would wish to distinguish three
types of meaning that can be conveyed in the uttering of a sentence.
In the first place we express our perceptions of events, processes,
states and abstractions. It is with this kind of meaning, together with
the meaning of lexical items, that semantics has been conventionally
concerned. It is what has been variously called 'ideational', 'cognitive'
or 'propositional' meaning.[1] In general it is the type of meaning that
is expressed through grammatical systems in different languages. In
the construction of any sentence the nature of the ideational meaning
that we wish to convey leads us to select an appropriate form for the
sentence. (I do not mean to imply that content and form are in any

---

[1] The term *ideational* is borrowed from M.A.K. Halliday: 'Functional
diversity in language'. *Foundations of Language.* 6 1970. Halliday's three-fold
division of 'functions' does not parallel the division into three types of meaning
that is proposed here.

way separable). It is evident that fundamental to our purpose in producing an utterance is the ideational meaning that we thereby convey. It appears that although the precise meanings and certainly the forms that express them vary between languages, similar types of meaning are expressed in many different languages. In Indo-European languages at least there is a significant interaction between these types of meaning and grammatical systems, so that equivalent systems among different languages can be identified without much difficulty. In fact it seems likely that any conclusions about the *types* of ideational meaning expressed through the grammar of language have wider validity and may be universal, however much the related systems may differ in detail. It is because of the close relationship between semantics and grammar, that it is feasible to approach decisions about grammatical forms to be taught through semantics. In any teaching that is limited in its aims, the limitation could well be designed to ensure that the learner at least has the means to convey certain fundamental meaning distinctions. In the semantic framework that is set out below, these types of meaning are brought together under the heading *semantico-grammatical* categories.

While expressing his perceptions the speaker simultaneously expresses his own attitude towards what he is saying (or writing). He vouches for the degree of validity that his statement has. He may represent it as simply an objective truth. On the other hand he may indicate that the ideational meaning is subject to some contingency, is desired rather than positively asserted or is potential rather than actual. In this case it is not asserted that an event has taken place or will take place; there is instead a degree of likelihood that it did so or will do so and this likelihood varies according to the type and degree of contingency. There is great variety in the linguistic devices that languages possess to express this kind of meaning which is here called *modal* meaning, or *modality*. In the first place it may be marked grammatically, lexically or phonologically (through intonation, for example). But even the grammatical categories themselves can be extremely varied. These may be a distinct category of modal particles, different moods of the verb (subjunctive, optative, jussive, for example), a class of modal verbs (as in English) or modal uses of some of the tenses in the basic verb paradigm (conditional, past).

The third type of meaning conveyed by an utterance is a matter of the function of the sentence (utterance) as a whole in the larger context in which it occurs. A sentence does more than communicate information. When it is uttered, it performs a role both in relation to other utterances that have been produced and as part of the interactive processes involving the participants. An account of the internal grammatical relations and therefore of the ideational meaning does not tell us much about the *use* to which a sentence is being put by the speaker. The speaker's purpose is no less a matter of what he is *doing* with the language than of what he is *reporting* through it. Although questions of use have not always been considered part of semantics, they are of great relevance to the language teacher who is preparing his pupils for the process of communication. However, while there has been quite enough scholarly discussion of semantics and grammatical categories for there to be little that is contentious in a list of candidates for inclusion in the semantico-grammatical inventory, there is no comparable authority for establishing a universal set of categories of language use. The more original part of the framework set out below, therefore, is in those categories, here called *categories of communicative function,* which are intended to handle the use of language. Whether it can be claimed that these categories are, in fact, universal is uncertain. Once one goes beyond a limited number of very broad categories into ever more subtle distinctions of language use, it becomes more and more likely that the distinctions are limited to the particular language being investigated. This does not mean that they are without relevance to language learning. On the contrary, part of a learner's task must be to approximate more and more to the language uses characteristic of the community whose language he is acquiring. There may therefore be some doubt as to the generality of some of the minor categories set out below, but, since the exemplification here is through English, there need be no doubt as to their potential importance for the learner of English.

It would perhaps be as well at this point to make certain aspects of terminology clear. Three different types of meaning have been distinguished and we have designated as a *notional syllabus* any strategy of language teaching that derives the content of learning from an initial analysis of the learner's need to express such meanings. We will find it convenient to refer to the categories of communicative function as expressing *functions or functional meaning,* (i.e. the social purpose of the utterance), whereas the semantico-grammatical categories express *concepts*[2] or *conceptional meaning* (i.e. the meaning relations expressed by the forms within the sentence). As we shall see in the last chapter (p. 68), it is correspondingly possible to think in terms of a *functional syllabus* and a *conceptual syllabus,* although only a syllabus that covered both functional (and modal) and conceptual categories would be a fully *notional syllabus*[3].

Although a fuller discussion of pedagogic questions is deferred until the final chapter, one or two points should be mentioned here. The inventory of notional categories that follows is intended as a tool in the construction of syllabuses. It does not itself constitute a notional syllabus. It sets out the categories that could usefully be drawn on by someone intending to produce such a syllabus. There is no pedagogic significance to the ordering of the categories in relation to one another nor to that of the sub-categories within the larger categories. It is a simple inventory arranged as far as possible in rational fashion. An actual notional syllabus would involve a process of selection and ordering from this larger inventory.

The fact that the categories are presented as an inventory is not meant to suggest that they are mutually exclusive. Any actual utterance inevitably contains many different kinds of grammatical meaning and may simultaneously perform more than one function. Looked at pedagogically, there is no way in which a single element of meaning (concept or language function) could be taught without other kinds of meaning simultaneously being introduced.

No attempt is made at full linguistic specification of the categories listed. Indeed they cannot be specified because often the facts are not adequately known, at least in the form in which they would need to be presented here. Instead, there is discussion of each category, sometimes with reference to pedagogic issues, brief exemplification

---

[2] If the individual units of meaning found within the semantico-grammatical section of the proposed framework are here referred to as concepts, this is only because some term is necessary in the ensuing discussion. In so far as individual concepts can be said to 'exist' at all, they are specific to particular languages. We can talk loosely about the supposed universality of 'the concept of time', but the actual time distinctions that people will be accustomed to producing and recognizing will be those that are reflected in the categories of their own language. While we shall find it useful to consider syllabus planning in terms of a logical division of time, we should not assume that individuals have an awareness of any such division independently of the perception of time that they derive from the categories of their own language.

[3] In this text the terms notional and semantic are regarded as largely synonymous and where the latter is used in such expressions as 'semantic needs', 'semantic demands' and 'semantic predictions', these are to be interpreted as referring to the philosophy of the notional approach as a whole and not to any one part of it. The use of the term semantic is therefore deliberately extended beyond what is conventionally held to be within the domain of the field of semantics. In this sense we might equally well refer to semantic as to notional syllabuses.

where a label might otherwise be unclear or a description alone inadequate, and occasionally more extensive exemplification in order to illustrate the linguistic and pedagogic implications of a semantic approach.

2.0 Semantico-grammatical categories

2.1.0 *Time*

In many, though not all, languages it is scarcely possible to produce a sentence without being involved in expressing time concepts. This is because tense systems tend to require choices based on time. We commonly indicate time by relating an event to the moment of utterance. In this sense, time might be considered partly a deictic category (see below p. 36-37)[4]. However for convenience both deictic and non-deictic aspects of time are considered together here.

2.1.1 *Point of time*

Although the importance and exact significance of time indicators varies according to culture, they are obviously an important part of the speaker's repertoire. The prominence given to expressions of time in language courses is a fair sign of this. Grammatically, points of time are usually expressed through adverbials:

e.g.   now, then
        on Monday the 23rd of April 1957
        at twenty-five past eight
        yesterday, today, tomorrow
        this/yesterday/to-morrow morning
        this/last/next month

It is interesting to note how many time expressions are deictic. That is to say, it is not possible to know the exact time referred to without knowing either the linguistic or the situational (temporal) context. While this is evident with expressions like *now, then, this morning*, it is not so apparent with *on Monday January 1st*. Yet in the context *I shall have a new car . . .*, this can only mean *next* January, that is the first January *after* the moment of utterance. In response to the question *when did you last see him?*, it would refer to January 1st *previous* to the moment of utterance. Even quite narrowly specified points of time can take the moment of utterance as their

---

[4] Deictic forms relate an utterance to its physical and linguistic context.

point of reference.

Time expressions are commonly taught as almost fixed phrases with limited productivity. However, points of time can equally be indicated through time clauses and through embedded sentences.

it must be finished when I come back
it must be finished by six o'clock
it must be finished by the time I leave

In these particular examples the time indicates the termination of an event, but it could equally mark its inception or the limits of its duration. The potential for embedding sentences in such time expressions offers a vast range of communicative potential, but, equally, an adequate competence exists even where a speaker has not mastered this kind of grammatical feature. It is likely that in a pedagogic ordering the embedded constructions would be deferred until later stages of learning.

2.1.2   Duration

The need to express periods of time may not be as essential as the need to express points of time, but languages nonetheless possess a range of resources which can be exploited for this purpose. A period of time may be denoted by explicit statement of its *duration* or by reference to its *inception* or *termination*. In English at least these distinctions are made by use of prepositional phrases:

e.g.   *for* five years
       until six o'clock
       since Monday
       from Monday

Lexical constructions are also possible including some which in a different context may refer to points of time:

e.g.   all the day
       the whole day
       this week
       last year

A comparable range of clausal constructions is available in English, introduced by such conjunctions as *while, when, since* and *until*. Expressions of points of time can be embedded to indicate the beginning or end of periods:

e.g.   she stayed at work until just before the clock struck seven

It is not unusual for languages to have the means of categorizing events as *punctual* or *durative* by grammatical devices. The progressive (be + -ing) form in English is sometimes described as a durative, although the present tense itself is only occasionally punctual. The

system of English requires the speaker to mark an event (verb) as durative or non-durative. A language like French expresses duration through periphrasis and the tense system posses forms which are not marked as either durative or non-durative:
periphrasis and the tense system possesses forms which are not marked as either durative or non-durative:

> e.g.   je lis
>   je suis en traîn de lire

2.1.3   *Time relations*

One of the major tasks that faces anyone learning a European language is acquiring the formal systems through which time relations are expressed. Events are placed in time by being related to the moment of speech and to time axes that have been established by other events. A characteristic of European languages is that these relations are expressed principally through verb forms (tenses), but this is not universally the case and there are many languages where verb forms are invariable and time relations are expressed by other devices.

In a notional approach we take a logical division of time as the starting-point. Such a division would need to go beyond a simple three-term system of *past, present* and *future,* since each of these may represent an axis in relation to which other events may be oriented. A system like the following, therefore, would be capable of handling more subtle time distinctions:

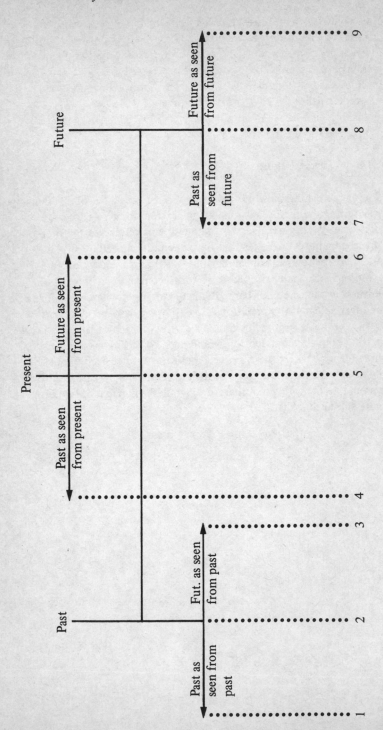

A speaker, with varying degrees of necessity, has to be able to express time relations of these kinds and a notional syllabus would be able to plan a progressive expansion in the learner's capacity to make time distinctions, probably ensuring that the broader distinctions were acquired first.

The problem in teaching is that such a time-scheme leads one to anticipate that languages will possess nine distinct verb forms whereas in fact they will probably possess fewer. To put it another way, in spite of the effort made by grammarians to squeeze actual verb systems into some such framework, the fact is that the *logical* organization of time is rarely directly reflected in the *grammatical* organization of time. Languages do not necessarily express a neat division into past, present and future, for example. (Nor are the forms in a verb paradigm uniquely concerned with time relations). English does not possess a future tense, although it has various ways in which future time can be referred to. In many languages the opposition past : present is much more clearly delimited than that of future : present. Present verb forms accept a future interpretation much more readily than a past interpretation, so that the opposition might be more accurately represented as past : present, future. Similarly, distinctions that can be made logically are often neutralized in the formal systems. Languages do not often make as many differentiations in regard to future as to past time. Frequently the same verb form will be used for 6, 8 and 9 above, for example. Not all languages are like English in their capacity to distinguish 2 (saw) and 4 (has seen).

The pedagogic advantage of approaching time relations logically is that, given that the ability to express time concepts is an important aspect of our communicative potential, we can ensure that the learner is provided with the linguistic means to express the most important time relations, whether or not the grammatical system is patterned along logical lines. A grammatical description of English will not identify a future verb form. But, in spite of the fact that futurity is expressed by forms that have other primary uses (present tense, present progressive, will + V) or by forms that do not enter the usual verb paradigm (going to + V), a notional approach would require that a learner be given some means of expressing futurity, since it is important for him communicationally. Paradoxically, since the language descriptions on which teaching is based often have a notional rather than a formal organization, (see above p. 18), it has usually been the practice in English teaching for some way of expressing the future to be included at quite an early stage of language learning.

Time relations are not uniquely expressed through verbs. Notions such as 'anterior to', 'posterior to' and 'simultaneous with' may be conveyed adverbially or by various combinations of grammatical forms. Adverbials introduced by such prepositions as *before, after, during* or conjunctions like *before, after* and *while,* make these relations explicit. A range of adjectives, nouns and adverbs provide lexical realizations of these concepts. A single example will show how, in English, verbal and non-verbal markers of time combine:

They sat looking at their watches. John would

arrive $\begin{cases} \text{at 8 o'clock.} \\ \text{before 8 o'clock.} \\ \text{after 8 o'clock.} \end{cases}$

The *would* establishes that the event is future in relation to the past time axis established by *sat*; the prepositions establish how the event relates to a specific point in time.

2.1.4   *Frequency*

Expressions of frequency or repetition vary from the most general to the most specific. A set of frequency adverbs in English expresses a gradation from *never* to *always*. No doubt all languages possess such expressions but they will certainly not necessarily make frequency distinctions identical to those found in English. More precision is obtained when specific time expressions are incorporated into frequency phrases:

    e.g. . . . on Mondays . . .
          . . . on some Mondays . . .
          . . . on the first Monday of each month . . .

As with other types of time expression these may contain embedded sentences:

    e.g. On days when it looks like raining, I go to work by car.
          Whenever it looks like raining, I go to work by car.

Whether or not verb forms will accept a frequentative interpretation depends on the language. In English the present tense usually marks the event as frequentative ('habitual'), but other forms of the English verb paradigm can also be used with frequentative meaning. More often, a language does not mark repetition in the verb, but through some specific lexical marker, as above, or through the context.

2.1.5   *Sequence*

Markers of sequence are, by definition, characteristic of types of continuous writing or speech. Ordinal numerals obviously have this function:

e.g.   first, second, third . . .
So do other adverbials and adjectives:
e.g.   then, next,finally . . .
        the next point is . . .
Sequence of events can be indicated simply by the order of clauses:
He came into the room and switched on the light.
He switched on the light and came into the room.

2.2.0   Quantity

2.2.1   Divided and undivided reference

It seems to be a universal characteristic of language that entities are
regarded as divisible or indivisible (countable or uncountable). In
consequence things may be represented as quantifiable or unquantifi-
able. Indeed the categorization of things on this dimension is not
fixed, since something that is regarded as uncountable in one context
may be regarded as countable in another. Quantification may be
marked formally in a number of different ways. Grammatical number
(usually singular/plural, but in some relatively exotic languages
singular/dual/plural), with few exceptions, operates on quantifiable
nouns (or, to be more accurate, nouns in a quantifiable sense):
e.g.   education   v. house
        educations* v. houses
Grammatical number, except in some anomalous cases, coincides
with notional number. We do usually use plural forms to refer to more
than one thing. Choice of article may depend on the status of the
noun, as in English:
e.g.   *language* is an essential characteristic of man
As this is a case of undivided reference, no article is selected. The use
of the indefinite artice, *a language*, would mean that one among many
languages was referred to.
   A continuum of more precise quantification can be expressed by
means of pre- and post-determiners:
e.g.   all, some, few, no etc.
In some cases the same quantifiers are used in English for both divided
and undivided reference, the difference being indicated by grammatical
number:
e.g.   all of the wine, a lot of wood
        all of the wines, a lot of friends
But sometimes different quantifiers have to be used:
e.g.   a little milk
        a few cows

Some nouns, though not themselves marked for plurality, require countable quantifiers and take plural concord:
    e.g.   many people like watching football
Languages do not necessarily classify entities in identical fashion but the similarities are far more striking than the differences.

It is also possible to regard *events* in terms of divided and undivided reference. *Aspect* in Russian is describable in these terms, perfective aspect referring to events seen as complete, (divided reference), imperfective aspect referring to events seen as incomplete (undivided reference). Aspect in English (be + -ing) could be regarded in the same way as essentially a type of quantification of events. Certainly many analyses do not accept that it is a durative form.

2.2.2   Numerals

Cardinal numbers enter into our communication at all levels and are obviously essential material in language learning.

2.2.3   Operations

The expression of mathematical operations is not of the greatest importance in foreign language learning for the general learner. Low-level calculations of the kind 'Ten and twelve make twenty-two', or 'Ten times twelve is a hundred and twenty', are likely to suffice for most learners. Obviously this category assumes much greater import-ance for specialized learners expecting to operate in fields which call for extensive use of mathematical concepts.

2.3.0   Space

2.3.1   Dimensions

The expression of dimensions can be an extremely important aspect of some specialized uses of language. The notion goes well beyond such things as linear dimensions and weight to include, for example, volume, gravity, elasticity, moisture, temperature etc. Where a language is being taught for special purposes, the nature of the subject will define the types of dimensions that need to be expressed. For the more general learner a course would seek to include those kinds of measurements which feature in everyday language use — distance, height, weight, speed etc.

2.3.2 *Location*

Location is most characteristically expressed through the use of prepositions, often associated with case inflection of nouns, though sometimes locative notions are expressed by cases without the use of prepositions. Locational concepts are often found in other word-classes:

e.g. verbs — *inhabit*

The distribution of prepositions varies a good deal from language to language and the prevalence of polysemy makes a notional approach difficult. There seems little point in attempting to establish a 'logical' system of locative notions although certain general notions are similar if not identical in many languages. In fact it is this generality which could be the key in a notional approach. Some prepositions have a more general distribution and even act almost as superordinate terms in relations to other prepositions. Preference might well be given to such terms.

e.g. (in English)   in, on, at, near
    cf.   inside, upon, behind, in front of . . .
    cf.   along, against, beyond, underneath . . .

2.3.3 *Motion*

One of the difficulties in dealing with spatial concepts is that most languages distinguish formally between static location and motion or direction, but that they do not do so consistently. Sometimes the same form may have both a locative and a directional sense; sometimes there are distinct forms for each. The pattern will vary from language to language. Where there is a case system, the case 'governed' by the preposition may vary according to whether or not motion is involved. In English, whereas all the locative prepositions mentioned above may occur in statements of movement, a number of prepositions can be used only where motion is involved. As above, in a process of limitation preference might be given to the more general:

e.g. to, from, in, on
cf.   towards, out of, into, on to . . .
cf.   across, off, down, past, through . . .

It is likely that comparable notions to these most 'general' English notions can be found in other languages, but that equivalents for the more limited ones will be more difficult to find. It is not without significance that these same prepositions are used for temporal as well as spatial location, often in a way that is semantically not unrelated to their spatial meaning. They also serve to express grammatical relations

which are not locative in character:
> e.g.   the passengers began *to* leave
> he believes *in* private enterprise

2.4.0   Relational Meaning

An important part of our communication involves the identification of entities (or reified abstractions) and the expression of relations between them. Although there are philosophical difficulties, it is supposed here that whatever our language background, we see certain things in much the same way however differently we may report them in the various languages we speak. Although the meanings covered here are expressed by means of syntactic relations, the categories themselves are taken to be semantic and hence relevant in the generally semantic approach adopted here. It is their expression in different languages that is a matter of syntax.

2.4.1   Sentential relations

The 'logical' relations that exist between nouns and between nouns and verbs in sentences are called 'case' relations by Fillmore[5]. (Halliday attempts to deal with the same kind of data under the heading of 'transitivity functions[6].) According to Fillmore they 'comprise a set of universal, presumably innate, concepts which identify certain types of judgement human beings are capable of making about the events that are going on around them, judgements about such matters as who did it, who it happened to and what got changed'. The five categories of relation that are suggested here are not exhaustive, but it is claimed that they enable useful statements to be made about semantic relations. It is possible to discover even finer distinctions, especially where the forms of particular languages are taken into account. But it is doubtful whether these have sufficient generality for there to be much value in including them here.

2.4.1.1   Agent

The agent is the usually animate entity carrying out the action represented by the verb:

---

[5] Fillmore C.J.: The case for case. In Bach E. and R.T. Harms (eds.) *Universals in Linguistic Theory.* New York. Holt, Rinehart. 1968.
[6] Halliday M.A.K.: Notes on transitivity and theme in English. Journal of Linguistics. 3/1 1967.

e.g. *John* drank the wine.
The wine was drunk by *John.*
It was *John* who drank the wine.
Without further differentiation the notion *agent* would also have to
be taken to include the grammatical subject in the following sentence:
A tile broke the window.

2.4.1.2 *Initiator*

The initiator is responsible for the action being performed but is not
actually the agent. Rather, the initiator causes something to be done:
e.g. *John* boiled the milk.
The nurse exercised her patients.
The patients were exercised by *the nurse.*

2.4.1.3 *Object*

The object is the entity acted upon or affected by the process
indicated by the verb:
e.g. John opened *the door.*
The door opened.
The door was opened by John.
Various kinds of object could be distinguished:
goals e.g. He touched *her arm.*
results e.g. Mary is knitting *a sweater.*

2.4.1.4 *Beneficiary*

The beneficiary is the animate being affected by or benefiting by the
process indicated by the verb:
e.g. They gave *John* a pay-rise
John was given a pay-rise.
She received a present.
He changed a pound for *his wife.*

2.4.1.5 *Instrument*

The instrument is the inanimate means by which an action is carried
out:
e.g. *The key* opened the door.
John used *the key* to open the door.
John opened the door with *the key*
Given that a major part of communication is concerned with

expressing meanings of this kind, to learn a language is to acquire a mastery of the formal means by which they are expressed. As soon as sentences are acquired, some familiarity with these notions is established. It is hard to imagine any course that does not see to it that the learner has some way of conveying *who* did *what* to *whom* with *what result* and so on. The significance in language teaching lies first in the fact that not all languages express these things in the same way. How many languages permit an instrument to occur (with certain verbs) as grammatical subject as English does? Secondly, each language allows the same semantic roles to be realized by several different syntactic functions. The examples above illustrate this. The question of what leads to the choice of one sentence form rather than another is highly significant. The choice depends on a combination of factors: the relation between the sentence in question and others that precede it, the emphasis or prominence to be given to the different parts, the distinction between what is already known and what is new, the type of text in which the sentence occurs. Without an awareness of the similarity in the underlying semantic functions that different forms of sentence may contain, there is no way of controlling them and relating them to one another.

2.4.2   *Predication and attribution*

Our perceptions of the world are further reflected in our predicating attributes and properties of objects. This is most significantly done in two ways. First there are predicative sentences like the following:

> e.g.   John is fat.
> John is my wife's brother.
> John is a pilot.
> Pilots are skilful.

It is common in English to talk about the predicative use of adjectives, but it is worth remembering that there are languages, like Japanese, where an English adjective would normally be translated as a verb.

The other way of assigning attributes is through structures of modification:

> e.g.   a *fat* man
> a man *with a long face*
> a man *who doesn't like flying*

2.5.0   *Deixis*

Languages appear to be universally capable of expressing deictic meaning. By deictic meaning is meant the capacity to refer an

utterance to the context in which it occurs. The context in this case
is both the linguistic and the non-linguistic context and what is
particularly significant is that, as will be seen below, the same
linguistic forms are used to refer to things within the act of speech
(*anaphora*) as are used to refer to things outside it. The reference
process most commonly relates to time, place and person.

2.5.1 *Time*

When *time* was discussed above it was pointed out that it expresses
deictic meaning. This means that as far as non-linguistic context is
concerned, events reported are related in time to the moment of
speech. Equally events are related to other events that have been
reported and this is deixis 'within language'. Some adverbials are
clearly deictic: *now, then, formerly, presently*. (Otherwise see 1.1 and
1.3 above).

2.5.2 *Place*

Orientation in space is regularly handled by use of demonstratives.
English has a two-term system to indicate relative proximity, *this/that
man*, but some other languages possess three demonstratives. Articles
can be regarded as at least partly deictic and indeed this is not
surprising since in many languages they are historically derived from
demonstratives:
    e.g. Shut *the* door!
Adverbial expressions are also found, *here* and *there*, for example.
However these are scarcely used anaphorically whereas the demonstratives and articles are:
    e.g. the use of *these* two lines above
        I saw a play yesterday . . . *the* play was a disaster
Other items used for within-text reference in English are *the former/
the latter* and *below/above* (in academic papers).

2.5.3 *Person*

In many languages there is no clear distinction between demonstrative
and personal pronouns and indeed these and articles are often very
closely related to one another. Pronoun systems are widely divergent,
but obviously are essential for even the most rudimentary communication. Person deixis also appears in the form of possessives, emphatic
pronouns and in verb inflection. Even where forms in different
languages appear similar, they are rarely exactly congruent. English *he,*

she and *it* which may be used to refer to objects and persons in the
situational context and to nouns according to sex (not gender) in the
linguistic context, are not directly comparable to *er, sie* and *es* in
German where selection is on the basis of gender (grammar). More
complex systems of pronouns are familiar in many more exotic
languages.

Paralleling the ostensive use of the pronouns in relation to the
situational context:

e.g.   *he* stole the purse   (pointing)

is the anaphoric use within the linguistic context:

e.g.   I saw John yesterday. *He* tells me *he's* going abroad.

3.0   Categories of modal meaning

3.1   *Modality*

As we saw above, a modal sentence is one in which the truth of the
predication is subject to some kind of contingency or modification.
It may not be asserted that something *is* (was) so, but that there is an
obligation, a necessity, a possibility or an intention that it should be
so (should have been so). So varied is the nature of the modal meanings
expressed in different languages that it is by no means certain that
there is much in common semantically between some of the forms that
are often labelled *modal.* In the formal analysis of modal verb systems
it has been common to distinguish two distinct types (uses) of
modality. In one case we have a scale of possibility, in the other what
might be called a scale of obligation. Jespersen points out that the
same verbs can be used in English to express necessity, possibility and
impossibility on the one hand and command, permission and prohibi-
tion on the other.[7] Other linguists have called these *logical* and *moral,*
or *epistemic* and *non-epistemic* respectively. The distinction is
maintained here but with modifications that are explained below.

3.1.1   *Scale of certainty*

This scale involves the speaker's report of the likelihood of the
predication being valid. Any such report is inevitably based on the
speaker's personal assessment of the facts, but a distinction is drawn
here between those judgements which are represented as objective
and those which are explicitly presented as personal. The difference

---

[7] O. Jespersen: *The Philosophy of Grammar.* London. Allen and Unwin.
1924. p 325.

between these two can be illustrated by the difference between *It is
certain that* . . . and *I am certain that* . . .or between *he must have
made at least a couple of million on the deal* and *I am convinced that
he made at least a couple of million on the deal.* The latter are largely
lexical in expression.

3.1.1.1 *Impersonalized*

Affirmation — this is not strictly part of the modal system as such and
is expressed by unmodalized, declarative sentences.
Certainty — i.e. certainty deduced
  e.g. He must be sixty if he is a day.
      He is certain to be there.
      It is inevitable that there will be a violent outcome.
Probability
  e.g. It is likely that I shall be able to play.
      I should be able to play.
      He ought to be able to play.
Possibility
  e.g. It may be a good programme.
      It is possible that the bus will be late.
      He is not certain to be there.
Nil certainty
  e.g. He is certain not to be there.
      It is not possible for her to go to college.
      It can't be true.
Negation — again, not truly part of the modal system, expressed by
negative declarative sentences.

3.1.1.2 *Personalized*

This section consists largely of a list of lexical items. They are
collected into four groups roughly paralleling the four groups of the
previous section, because on the whole sentences with these lexical
items imply the degrees of possibility expressed above. It is not of
course suggested that items grouped together have identical meaning.
Conviction — believe, be + convinced, positive, confident, sure, certain
  e.g. I believe there will soon be a change of government.
      I am sure they will win.
Conjecture — think, presume, suppose, infer, daresay, expect, judge,
conclude, trust, be of the opinion, assume, hold, suspect, subscribe (to
the view that), anticipate, foresee, predict, prophesy, consider, reckon,
hope, surmise, guess, imagine, conjecture.

e.g.   I think it's going to rain.
       I expect I'll see you there.
Doubt — doubt, wonder, be + sceptical, doubtful, dubious
e.g.   I doubt whether there is much hope for them.
       I am sceptical about the chances of a successful outcome.
       I don't suppose he'll be on time.
       I am not convinced that he is telling the truth.
Disbelief — above verbs + negative
e.g.   I don't believe he will be there.
       I believe that he won't be there.
       I am convinced that he is not telling the truth.
       I don't think it is worth waiting.

It is worth noting that although in the English examples here the modality is expressed lexically, in French a subjunctive form of the verb would be necessary in some of the subordinate clauses. In general this would be true of sentences equivalent to the last two groups, which are negatively oriented.

e.g.   Je ne crois pas qu'il soit là.

Not dissimilar is German where the reliability of the proposition in the embedded clause can be made explicit by using the subjunctive or the indicative:

Er denkt, dass sein Freund gekommen *sei*. (Subjunctive)
Er denkt, dass sein Freund gekommen *ist*. (Indicative)
He thinks that his friend came.

The implication of the choice of the subjunctive is that his friend did not in fact come, whereas, in the case of the indicative, the friend did indeed come. The wishes and intentions of the next section are also followed by subjunctives in some languages.

3.1.2   *Scale of commitment*

This scale deals with that aspect of modality that enables us to report degrees of moral undertaking and responsibility, whether on our own or on someone else's part. As examples of this we can cite such sentences as *I/he must be there by six* or *I/he'll be there by six*. In some cases reporting and undertaking/imposing the commitment may be done with exactly the same form of sentence. In the latter case the verbs are acting essentially as performatives (see p.43). These are Jespersen's commands, permissions and prohibitions. In spite of the formal similarities, they are here deferred, to be included with other kinds of speech act under *Suasion* (see p. 46). The difference between describing a commitment (obligation) and imposing it (command) is frequently, but not exclusively, a matter of changing the subject pronoun. The obligations reported in the two examples above could become commands if we changed the subject: *you must be there by six* or *you will be there by six*. This would be particularly the case with sentence stress on *will*. Use of the largely archaic *shall* would have the same effect: *you shall be there by six*.

3.1.2.1 *Intention*

The following lexical items all relate to the subject's intent with regard to a proposition. Most of them can be used in utterances expressing intention: will, volition, choice, inclination, intention, purpose, wish, desire, unwilling, design, mean, propose, contemplate, plan, project, want, prefer, promise, undertake, assure, guarantee, contract
   e.g. I'll pick you up at the station.
          I may drop in for a drink.
          He intends to stay at home this evening.
          I prefer to buy a new car.

3.1.2.2 *Obligation*

duty, liability, responsiblity, allegiance, conscientiousness, obligation, onus
   e.g. They must pay up by the end of the week.
          He ought to stop and help.
          We are liable for the entire cost.
          I need not resign my job.
          The onus is on me to sort it out.
          I've got to sort it out.

4.0   Categories of communicative function

The categories of this part of the framework are based on the third type of meaning described above, the meaning that arises from the fundamental distinction, very important for language teaching, between what we *do* through language and what we report by means of language. For example, the person who says, 'The manager ordered the drunk out of the restaurant' is *reporting* what took place (a command). The person who says, 'Get out of here' or 'Time you left' is *issuing* a command. The fact that we may know (in the case of a foreign language) how to report does not mean that we know how to do. In this case, 'I order you out of this restaurant' is a possible but very unlikely way of issuing a command. Where a report might be expressed as 'The manager threatened to call the police', the act of threatening itself could be 'If you don't get out, I'll call the police', and *not* 'I am threatening to call the police'.

Language learning has concentrated much more on the use of language to report and describe than on doing things through language. This is because the learning of lexical labels (command, threat, warning, surprise . . .) has been substituted for the learning of how the acts themselves are performed and because grammatical categories have too often been taken as categories of communication too. (Imperative = command, Interrogative = question, Comparative = comparison . . .)

The whole basis of a notional approach to language teaching derives from the conviction that what people want to do through language is more important than mastery of the language as an unapplied system. While *reporting* and *describing* are acts that we would like to carry out through language and which we can perform largely with a knowledge of the semantico-grammatical categories, they are by no means the only ones that are important for the learner of a foreign language. In this section a categorization is proposed for assigning utterances to particular functions. The categories are not restricted to acts of the kind that have been mentioned so far, nor do they limit themselves to what have come to be called *speech acts.*[8] They include some categories needed to handle cases where there is no one-to-one relation between grammatical category and communicative function and others involving expression of the speaker's intention and views.

The framework adopted is largely *ad hoc.* To be entirely satisfying a multi-dimensional approach would have been necessary, since there are many components to the distinctions between the different functions. To have developed a theory to handle these distinctions exhaustively and without redundancy would have been a considerable distraction from the essentially practical task in hand. The categories do therefore to some extent overlap one another and some functions could be placed equally well within more than one category in the system.

In the places where I have attempted to suggest some possible linguistic realizations of the communicative functions, the suggestions are made on the basis of introspection and not as the result of objec-tive, observational research. In fact, research into the realization of different functions is a task that would occupy many linguists

---

[8] As in, for example, J.R.Searle: *Speech Acts.* Cambridge, Cambridge University Press. 1970.

for many years. Rather than insist that practical applications of these ideas should await the results of long-term research. I have preferred a more speculative, subjective approach which can be of some immediate practical value.

There are some general linguistic points to be made before we look at the categories in detail:

(*a*)   From what has already been said, it will be clear that it is not simply a matter of adding thousands of lexical items to the learner's store. A thesaurus shows thousands of words which relate to and label these functions. By no means all, and perhaps not even most of them are used in performing these functions. In the same way, there will be no single, unambiguous, grammatical structure by which a function is realized.

(*b*)   Broadly, we are more concerned with what the speaker intends to achieve than with the effect he may inadvertently or indirectly have. The effect of one speaker's utterances may be to *bore* his hearers, but it would be foolish and irrelevant to look for the linguistic means by which one succeeds in boring one's hearers. To use Austin's terms, we are concerned with *illocution* and not *perlocution*. [9]

(*c*)   There is a class of verbs, the utterance of which seems to constitute the act itself:

   e.g.   I pronounce you man and wife.

   I promise to be here by twelve.

By no means all acts involve *performatives* of this sort and even where they are available, they are rarely the sole means of expression. Use of the relevant noun or a performative verb is often limited to more formal occasions.

(*d*)   It must not be assumed that where the relevant noun or verb is used, the function of the utterance is automatically to be identified with it:

   e.g.   I *question* your motives.

   I *state* that I was not responsible for the accident.

The former is not a *question* and the latter might be labelled *emphatic assertion* rather than *statement*.

(*e*)   The same word may be used in both reporting and performing a linguistic act:

   e.g.   He promised to come.

   I promise to come.

We are here concerned with the latter, but since the syntactic features are the same in each case, it is clear that in these instances learning to

---

[9] J.L.Austin: *How to do Things with Words.* Oxford. Clarendon Press. 1962.

make a promise is also learning to *report* a promise, and vice versa. In cases like this we might allow this pedagogic advantage to influence us in deciding which realization of *promising* we would wish to teach.
(*f*)   Few of the acts with which we are concerned have a unique means of linguistic expression. Some may contain a performative element. There will be some almost formulaic expressions in which simple substitution of lexical items is possible. In some cases particular grammatical categories will be closely associated with the communicative function. However, often,exact interpretation of an utterance will be impossible without knowledge of the situational and broader linguistic context. Intonation too plays a very important role in indicating the function of an utterance. Finally there are occasions when no linguistic means at all are used to indicate what is being communicated, (as when we shake our heads to express *disagreement*).
(*g*)   It is possible that a learner who already has an advanced knowledge of the lexical and grammatical systems of a language can himself go a long way towards inferring the communicative functions of utterances to which the systems are applied. He may not need to be taught how to interpret utterances. This could only be the case where his knowledge was really very advanced and even so there would be many cases where grammatical and lexical knowledge was not enough.

In the remaining part of this chapter six types of communicative function are recognized, six kinds of thing that we do with language. Within each a set of further sub-categories is established. With each of these a list of related lexical items is given. Some, but not all of these may constitute different acts of speech. Equally,although closely related to the semantic field of the communicative function, they may be used only in the process of reporting. From time to time exemplification is given of what might constitute realizations of a particular function.

4.1   Judgement and evaluation

This category deals with assessments and the subsequent expression of those assessments.

4.1.1   *Valuation*   estimate, value, assess, appreciate, judge, rank, place, grade
      overestimate, prejudge, misjudge.

4.1.2   *Verdiction*   pronounce, rule, sentence, find, award

4.1.2.1 *Committal* condemn, convict, proscribe

4.1.2.2 *Release* exempt, release, acquit, discharge, let off, excuse, pardon, conciliate, reconciliate, forgive, exculpate, exonerate, absolve, reprieve, extenuate

4.1.3 *Approval* (i.e. approval of another's behaviour, performance etc.) approbation, approve, think well, appreciate, commend, praise, applaud, value, deserve, merit, entitle, give credit

4.1.4 *Disapproval* disapprobation, deprecate, blame, remonstrate, reprimand, accuse, denounce, condemn, frown upon, disparage, charge, impute, reproach, deplore, allege, complain
We know very little of the way in which language is exploited in the performing of any of these functions. One thing that seems clear is that most of the verbs listed above can themselves act as performatives. As realizations of functions grouped here as giving *release* (from guilt), we could find such sentences as:
e.g. I acquit you of this charge.
      I discharge you from this case.
      I exonerate you from blame.
      I absolve you of guilt.
Each of these provides release in a fairly formal situation and this is often a characteristic of the use of performatives. But there is a virtually infinite number of ways in which the same communicative effect can be achieved without use of a performative and often with no lexical item related in meaning to any of those taken here to convey *release*.
e.g. You are free to go.
      I see nothing against him.
      You are not to blame.
      It wasn't your fault.
      It isn't your responsibility.

You are { blameless.
         { innocent.

I   { believe in.
         { accept.   his innocence.
         { etc.

      You can have a clear conscience.
      You are cleared of the charge.
Given the variety of ways in which the same effect might be achieved, the pedagogic problem would be to identify which was sufficiently generalizable to be of value to the language learner. In this instance, it

is not clear that any of the above sentences could be a basis for a wider generalization.

If we take another category, that of *blame*, we find a similar situation. How does one lay the blame on someone? The answer is first in the use of the lexeme BLAME in various sentences:

e.g.   I blame John.
       You are to blame / I am to blame.
       You'll have to take the blame.
       I put the blame on the doctor.

But there are even more ways of laying the blame explicitly with the use of other related lexical items:

e.g.   It's your fault.
       You are guilty.
       You have no excuse.

It was
$\left\{\begin{array}{l}\text{on account of}\\\text{the result of}\\\text{because of}\\\text{due to}\end{array}\right.$
your negligence.

That was completely unjustified.

Your behaviour is quite
$\left\{\begin{array}{l}\text{reprehensible.}\\\text{indefensible.}\\\text{inexcusable.}\\\text{unpardonable.}\end{array}\right.$

Or, more implicitly:
       I take strong exception to your behaviour.
(i.e. if I take exception to it, there must be something blameworthy in it)

Almost any reaction of pleasure to something done or said by someone else could be interpreted as implying *approval* and relatively transparent expressions such as *I approve of it very much* or, simply, *I like it* are not likely to be the most common ways of expressing approval.

4.2   *Suasion*

These are categories of utterance designed to affect the behaviour of others.

4.2.1   *Inducement* persuade, suggest, advise, recommend, advocate, exhort, beg, urge, incite, propose

4.2.2   *Compulsion* command, order, dictate, direct, compel, force, oblige, prohibit, forbid, disallow

4.2.3   *Prediction* warn, caution, menace, threaten, predict, instruct, direct, invite.

4.2.4   *Tolerance* (i.e. no hindrance offered to a proposal) allow, tolerate, grant, consent, agree to, permit, authorize.
The category of *suasion* contains a number of functions which are potentially of the greatest significance in language teaching. It is very much part of our aim in learning a language that we should be able to produce and understand suggestions, pieces of advice, commands, prohibitions, warnings, directions, invitations, permission and authorizations. The possible realizations of these categories can be illustrated by contrasting two closely associated functions, *suggesting* and *advising*. The contrast between the two is taken to be that while both propose a course of action, a suggestion does not carry the speaker's recommendation and has no implication of benefit for the hearer. In giving advice, on the other hand, one expresses an opinion that to follow it would be in the hearer's interest.

In the first instance there will be performative sentences:

(S)   I suggest   { a visit to the zoo.
                    that we go to the zoo.
                    that you go to the zoo.

(A)   I advise   { you to take the job.
                     that you take the job.
      I recommend   acceptance of the job
      I suggest strongly that you take the job.

Secondly there are grammatical expressions capable of generating many sentences/utterances having the same communicative function:

(S)   Shall we
      Let's
      Why don't we   } go to the zoo.
      You could
      You might

      How about   } (us)
      What about   (our) going to the zoo.
      Have you thought of

      Suppose   (went)
                   we   to the zoo.
      Supposing   (go)

      Another possibility } would be to go to the zoo.
      An alternative

(A)   The best course seems to be ⎫
       It seems advisable   ⎬ (for you) to take the job.
       It would be best   ⎭
       If you take my advice, you'll take the job.
       (If I may give you some advice,)   I would take the job.
       (If I were you,)   I would seriously consider
                                            taking the job.

       I think you should ⎫
       You'd better   ⎬ take the job.

       Under no circumstances ⎫
       On no account   ⎬ take the job.

       Don't take that job ⎧ under any circumstances.
                           ⎩ on any account.

Finally there are utterances which do not *express* the given function
but *imply* it:

(S)   I wonder ⎧ whether the zoo is open.
                 ⎩ if

       Perhaps the zoo is open.
       Would you consider going to the zoo.
       (Has anyone got a suggestion?) Well, there's the zoo.

(A)   Why don't you take the job?
       Do you think it's advisable? (i.e. with strong implications that
           it is not advisable.)

The lexical items listed under tolerance are obviously closely
related to one another and do not necessarily constitute distinct
functions. Most of the verbs can act as performatives and it is
interesting to note the differing syntactic possibilities even where the
verbs are related semantically:

       e.g.   ⎧ his visit to the prison.   i.
                               ⎪ him to visit the prison.   ii.
             I (hereby) authorize ⎨ that he should visit the prison. iii.
                               ⎩ his visiting the prison.   iv.

An identical range of complement structures is not permitted with the
other verbs:

allow	i.	ii.	iii.	
consent to	i.			iv.
agree to	i.			iv.
permit	i.	ii.		iv.
approve	i.		iii.	iv.
tolerate	i.			iv.

This illustrates how far advanced use of English is dependent on the
ability to handle this aspect of English grammar and how difficult it
must be for the learner to master the use of complement structures

when no semantic generalization can help him.

4.3   Argument

These categories relate to the exchange of information and views. There is a clear overlap between utterances which enter this category and those involved in *Suasion* (4.2) and *Rational enquiry and exposition* (4.4). The presentation of information can obviously be part of a larger suasive and expositive use of language. This brings us to an important point which has been obscured in the discussion so far. It is not to be assumed that each category of function listed here is automatically realized as a single sentence. It may be a longer stretch of language and this in turn makes it possible for one function to be contained within another. A set of instructions (Suasion) for the playing of a game may identify (Rational enquiry and exposition) the pieces or equipment need for the game. This should be borne in mind throughout, although, for convenience, exemplification will always be in the form of single sentences.

4.3.1   Information

4.3.1.1 *Asserted* tell, inform, report, proclaim, publish, assert, declare, state, emphasize, argue, know, affirm, maintain, advocate, claim, contend, protest

4.3.1.2 *Sought* request, question, ask

4.3.1.3 *Denied*, disprove, refute, negate, confute, deny, disclaim, refuse, oppose, decline, reject, protest, describe

4.3.2   Agreement

These are utterances which agree with a statement or proposal made. (cf. *agree to* (8.4)).
confirm, corroborate, endorse, support, assent, acquiesce, agree, concur, consent, ratify, approve

4.3.3   *Disagreement* dissent, demur, disagree, repudiate, contradict, dispute

4.3.4   *Concession*

This is the category of utterance which cedes an argument or with-
draws a case:
concede, grant, admit, yield, defer, renounce, withdraw, abjure,
abandon, retract, allow, confess, submit, resign, apologize
The functions in the category of *argument* are central to the
learner's purpose in acquiring a language. *Stating* is carried out
principally through declarative sentences and the actual form of these
statements will be determined by the semantico-grammatical meanings
to be expressed. *Asserting* is a matter of stating with conviction or
emphasis. In English we can assert by manipulating the intonation and
rhythm of a statement, but without otherwise changing its form. If we
look at sentences where the assertion is made explicit through use of
performative verbs or through other clearly marked forms, we will see
that *assertion* and *modality* are closely related:

    e.g.   I assert   ⎫
           contend   ⎪
           state   ⎪
           swear   ⎬   that I was not responsible for the accident.
           know   ⎪
           am sure   ⎪
           am certain   ⎪
           am convinced   ⎭

Of course there are plenty of other ways of asserting:

    e.g.   I don't want to appear dogmatic but I ⎫
                             I can tell you. I   ⎬   was not responsible.
                          You take it from me. I ⎭

Asking *questions* and making *requests* are two significant uses of
language for the learner. Questioning is obviously principally the use
of grammatically interrogative sentences, but it should not be forgot-
ten that questions can be asked using declarative sentences with
question intonation and that interrogative sentences do not always
serve as questions:

    e.g.   Why don't you try putting more fertilizer on. (*suggestion*)

Let us look more closely at *requests*. Making a request is here taken
to mean asking *that* something should be done or asking *for* something
(including information). It presupposes that the speaker wants something carried out. However, the speaker has no authority over the
addressee and therefore cannot give a command that it should be
done. Requests and *commands* are not always distinguished formally
from one another, since what appears to be a request may in fact have
all the strength of a command if the speaker has, or believes he has,

the necessary authority over the hearer. Intonation has an important role in marking requests.

The verb *request* can be used performatively:

e.g. I request you to leave the country.

Such an utterance would be restricted to very formal circumstances and in spite of the use of the verb *request*, it functions probably not as a request but as a command. There are, then, many, widely used ways of making requests:

e.g. Would you mind ⎫
               ⎬ shutting the window?
      Do you mind ⎭

Would you like to shut the window?

Could ⎫
Would ⎪
Will   ⎬ you
Can ⎭

Would ⎫   ⎧ so good as   ⎫   ⎫ shut the window?
     ⎬ you be ⎨ so kind as   ⎬ to ⎬
Will ⎭   ⎪ good enough ⎪   ⎭
              ⎩ kind enough ⎭

                ⎧ will you.
Shut the window, ⎨ would you.
                ⎩ please.

More idiomatically there are such utterances as:

May ⎫
     ⎬ I trouble you for a light?
Can ⎭

Have you got a light?

(It is worth noting that wheareas a probable reaction to the last utterance is a physical movement, perhaps accompanied by an utterance like 'Mm. Here you are,' the response to a similar interrogative like 'Have you got a freezer?' could be 'No, we don't think they're worth buying' or 'Yes, we've got a Frigidaire'. The second interrogative is therefore a *question* and not a *request*.)

Utterances which are requests by implication, but often quite unambiguously, are sentences like the following:

I wish you'd be quiet.

If you shut the window, we'll soon get warm.

You might shut the window.

Perhaps you'd like to shut the window.

I hoped you'd lend me a pound. (*not* past time)

In all these examples, it is interesting to note the recurrence of interrogatives, modal verbs and past tenses, all of which have the modal effect of rendering a proposition less direct.

A function like *disagreement* is probably more often performed quite implicitly. One disagrees with someone simply by expressing a different view from the one which the other person has just expressed. In practice, we often choose to avoid expressing disagreement bluntly:

e.g.

I disagree with $\begin{cases} \text{your argument.} \\ \text{you.} \\ \text{what you are saying.} \end{cases}$

I can't accept your argument.

I can't agree with you.

I $\begin{cases} \text{can't} \\ \text{don't} \end{cases}$ share your views.

I couldn't agree less.

That's $\begin{cases} \text{nonsense.} \\ \text{rubbish.} \end{cases}$

Utterances like these will be reserved for occasions when politeness is not necessary. On the whole where disagreement is made explicit, it is likely to be expressed in more gentle terms:

I beg to differ.

I $\begin{cases} \text{would} \\ \text{rather} \\ \text{tend to} \\ \text{would rather tend to} \end{cases}$ disagree with you.

The hearer can often readily infer the speaker's disagreement with him:

If you don't mind me saying so, there are certain factors you haven't taken into account.

I must say that I am not at all sure that what you are saying is true.

I see things rather differently.

4.4   *Rational enquiry and exposition*

This category relates to the rational organization of thought and speech. As has already been pointed out, utterances in this category interact with and possibly overlap those in the categories of *argument* and *suasion*. Drawing conclusions, making conditions, comparing and contrasting, defining, explaining reasons and purposes, conjecturing and verifying, inferring and implying are the very matter of communication, whether that communication be in the form of everyday conversation or more highly articulate and specialized uses of language. In much use of language these functions are to be inferred by the hearer:

e.g.   It's raining. I'm going to put my coat on. (*reason*)

In more formal writing and speech, it is normal for these functions to be marked explicitly and creating in the individual the ability to do this clearly and unambiguously is one of the major objectives of education.

e.g.   Because pensions have been increased, taxes must be raised.

A fairly substantial list of functions for inclusion in this category has been drawn up, but it is by no means certain that it is exhaustive and for this reason the functions have not been grouped in any way.

implication, deduction, supposition, conjecture, assumption, proposition, hypothesis, substantiation, verification, justification, proof, conclusion, demonstration, condition, consequence, result, inference, illation, corollary, presupposition, interpretation, explanation, definition, illustration, exemplification, concession, purpose, cause, reason, classification, comparison, contrast, generalization.

Traditional grammatical descriptions have always provided information on some of these meanings. Clauses of purpose and result, conditions and comparatives are grammatical forms identified by means of notional labels. Not that purposes, results, conditions and comparisons are necessarily expressed by the forms that carry these labels:

e.g.   I'd rather like to have that. The question is, have I got
          enough money?
          (= *condition* – I'd rather like to have that, if I've got enough
          money)
          Mary isn't bad looking, but Joanne is really pretty.
          (= *comparison* – Joanne is prettier than Mary)

Definitions are obviously a feature of scientific and other academic forms of writing. We do however make definitions, though informally, in every-day use of language:

e.g.   Thyme is a kind of herb used in cooking.

Scientific definitions are more elaborate, but not fundamentally different in structure:

e.g.   The atomicity of an element is the number of atoms
          contained in one molecule of the element.

The lexeme DEFINE does occur in definitions:

e.g.   A reversible reaction may be defined as a reaction which will
          proceed in either direction if conditions are arranged
          appropriately.

4.5   *Personal emotions*

The functions in this category express the speaker's emotional reactions to events and people.

4.5.1   *Positive* pleasure, enjoyment, satisfaction, delight, contentment, peace of mind, wonder, marvel, astonishment, admiration, surprise, amazement, fascination

4.5.2   *Negative* shock, displeasure, dissatisfaction, annoyance, irritation, care, anxiety, grief, sorrow, discontent, disappointment, bewilderment, anger, indignation, vexation, exasperation, resentment, lamentation, disdain, scorn, spite
   These categories are more or less self-explanatory. It need perhaps only be pointed out that to know the word *anger* is not to know how to express anger. It is also worth repeating that the above is a list of lexical items associated with the expression of positive and negative emotions. It must not be assumed that there are distinct ways of expressing each and that therefore each can be considered a different use of language. Obviously words like *pleasure, enjoyment, satisfaction* and *delight* are very closely related in meaning and it is unlikely that one could say that a given utterance expressed pleasure rather than enjoyment.

4.6   *Emotional relations*

These are largely *phatic* utterances expressing as they do various relationships with the person addressed.

4.6.1   *Greetings* welcome, greeting, salute, farewell

4.6.2   *Sympathy* solicitude, regret, concern, condolence, sympathy, tolerance, consideration, comparison, commiseration, consolation

4.6.3   *Gratitude* thankfulness, gratefulness, acknowledgement, thanks

4.6.4   *Flattery* compliment, flattery, obeisance

4.6.5   *Hostility* curse, execration, abuse, threat, damn, disdain, contempt, scorn, coolness, indifference

CHAPTER THREE

Applications of a Notional Syllabus

1.0   Introduction

Notional syllabuses as such do not, to my knowledge, exist. The argument of the first chapter is that a notional approach to syllabus design represents a strategy in the structuring of language learning that contrasts with the more common grammatical structuring. I have labelled this strategy *analytic* and the second chapter sets out in what is, I hope, more or less exhaustive fashion, the categories on which it would be necessary to draw in putting such a strategy into practice. The potential of the notional syllabus as a structure for language teaching is obviously still largely unexplored. There is, therefore, all the more need for some discussion of the way in which it might be operated and of the pedagogic implications that it seems to carry.

2.0   The forms of a notional syllabus

The essence of a notional syllabus will be in the priority it gives to the semantic content of language learning. The first step in the construction of any language syllabus or course is to define objectives. Wherever possible these will be based on an analysis of the needs of the learners and these needs, in turn, will be expressed in terms of the particular types of communication in which the learner will need to engage. The categories of the preceding chapter are intended to make it possible for questions about the types of communication to be formulated in fairly precise terms. It need hardly be said that there is no way in which the actual meanings that people will want to express can be predicted. But this is no different from what happens with the grammatical approach. One cannot predict the actual forms of sentences that people will need to produce, but this does not prevent one from arming the learner with a knowledge of the general rules of the grammatical system so that he can create the sentences as needed. In a notional approach the aim is to ensure that the learner knows how different types of meaning are expressed, so that he can then adapt and combine the different components of this knowledge according to the requirements of a particular act of communication.

The principal difficulty in applying a notional approach stems from the fact that there is no one-to-one relation between grammatical forms and either grammatical meanings (conceptual meaning) or language functions. Exactly the same problem inevitably arises in a grammatical approach, but in that case it is rarely recognized. Where semantico-grammatical and modal meanings are concerned, there is, in English, no single realization for such notions as *future time, agent* or *possibility*. Any logical set of spatial relationships can only with difficulty be mapped on to the linguistic forms (e.g. prepositions) that actually express the relationships. However the lack of congruence between form and meaning is most striking in the case of functional meaning, that is, in the use of sentences as utterances in actual acts of speech. An individual sentence can be used to perform virtually any function in the language and consequently any function may take a variety of forms.

If we know nothing of the context we would imagine an utterance like 'It's raining', to be an example of the type of communication that is usually called *phatic communion.* The aim of the speaker is not so much to convey a piece of information as to establish a relationship with the person he is addressing. Talking about the weather is one way of doing this. However, if we were to supply an appropriate context, we could readily show that the same form might equally serve as a *suggestion* or a *refusal.* If it was addressed to somebody who was about to leave the front door of a house, it could have the meaning, 'I suggest that you take an umbrella or put on your raincoat.' Said by a mother whose child has just asked whether he can go and play in the garden, it means, 'No, you can't'.

This would seem to imply that one cannot make generalizations about the forms of sentences and their use as utterances. If this was so, it would be a grave flaw in the argument in favour of semantic syllabuses. No one could conceivably propose that *it is raining* should be taught as a *way* of making suggestions. Language teaching depends upon our ability to make generalizations about language structure, otherwise language learning would be the acquisition of individual sentences or utterances and the learner would only develop his linguistic creativity very slowly and inefficiently. In the case of the grammar, one achieves generalization by focussing on the most *productive* aspects of the grammatical system, aspects where on the basis of a few examples a rule can be formulated which then applies very widely through the language. In the case of the functional aspects of language, one looks for a recurrent association between a given function and certain linguistic features. It proves that, in spite of the

fact that particular functions *may* be realized in almost any way that
suits the context, there are conventional interpretations that would be
put upon sentences in the absence of contextual information that
would contradict them. It is for this reason that people use grammatical labels like *interrogative* and functional labels like *question*
more or less interchangeably. Interrogatives *are* used as questions,
though not exclusively. Similarly utterances like, 'Have you got a
light, pencil, screwdriver . . .' are readily understood as requests for
lights, pencils and screwdrivers and not as information questions.
Conventions of use do exist and it is these that would be exploited in
the construction of a notional syllabus.

It can now be seen that the process of selection which is inevitably
involved in the construction of language teaching programmes will, in
the case of a notional syllabus require not only a choice of the types
of meaning to be learned (and *when* they should be learned), but also
by what linguistic forms those meanings are to be expressed. The
choice between the different grammatical structures by which one
function may be realized will be largely determined by the exact
sociolinguistic (or stylistic) conditions under which communication
is taking place. It follows, therefore, that the criteria developed over
the years for the operation of grammatical and situational syllabuses
are by no means irrelevant even in a notional syllabus. They may no
longer be the first considerations but they may still help determine
which linguistic form should be taught at a particular stage. The
adoption of a notional syllabus, therefore, does not necessarily imply
the abandonment of well-established criteria. Rather the familar
criteria are to be incorporated into a new, notional framework.

One of the consequences of adopting a notional approach is a far
greater sensitivity to the differing conditions under which language
teaching takes place. The precise interaction of semantic, situational
and grammatical factors will vary according to these circumstances.
We can make these conditions explicit in the form of a number of
questions. Are the learners aiming for a general or a specialized
language competence? Is the course extensive or intensive? Is it a
short- or long-term course? Is the ultimate goal some limited proficiency in the language or is it intended to proceed until native-like
proficiency is achieved? Will the language be required for use during
the period of learning or only at the terminal point? Are the learners
absolute beginners or is the course at least partly remedial? Are the
learners adults or children? The answers to these and other questions
will influence the precise form that the syllabus takes and will change
the weighting of different criteria that might be used. It is for this
reason that this section is entitled *the forms of a notional syllabus*,

with the implication that there is no unique or ideal notional syllabus
to be established. In this, I believe the notional syllabus to be largely
in contrast with a grammatical syllabus. The latter tends to be very
similar whatever the answers to the above questions (except perhaps
that on specialized use). The syllabus consists of a linear progression
of the most significant grammatical structures, albeit with possible
variation in the steepness of the grading and the location of the end-
point. In other ways the content of learning is not specially adapted
to the conditions of learning. Because of this inherent variability in
the conditions of learning, the following discussion is devoted more to
demonstrating the differing ways in which semantic considerations
might influence syllabus design than to attempting to establish a fixed
and universal set of relationships between semantic, situational and
grammatical features.[1]

2.1   Global course design

We can best consider some of the general issues that arise in connection
with notional syllabuses by looking at how they might be adopted in
the provision of general courses, that is to say, courses intended for
beginners aiming to proceed towards a general and fairly high proficiency in the language.

A linear organization cannot as easily be adopted in a notional
syllabus as in a grammatical syllabus. Indeed, even in the case of a
grammatical approach it is rather naive to think that each unit in the
sequence deals with only one grammatical structure at a time. Any
new grammatical category is presented in the context of a whole
sentence and that sentence may obviously contain other grammatical
features than the one that is the immediate objective of the unit. They
may even be features that have not yet been taught. In the same way
that a grammatical defined unit cannot be confined to a single grammatical point, a semantically defined unit cannot be limited to a
single type of meaning. Any utterance or type of utterance that is

---

[1] Certain of the factors that affect syllabus design derive from the objectives
of the course and the conditions under which it is taking place. For this reason
the following discussion is arranged according to the types of course envisaged
(global, specialized, intensive, short-term etc). This arrangement is not intended
to suggest that some of the issues raised under the heading of, say, global course
design are not equally relevant for other kinds of courses. Furthermore, it is
evident that a remedial course, for example, may also have 'global' objectives or
may be intensive and of limited duration. The separation does, however, permit
the issues to be more clearly identified.

taught will express a certain constellation of conceptual meanings and will simultaneously perform one or more functions in the larger context. It may also be marked for modality. An utterances cannot simply be an expression of *time,* or of a *request* or of *possibility.* It could easily express all three within the same utterance: *Could you possibly tell me when time is up?*

However, in spite of the similarity of grammatical and semantic content in this respect, a notional syllabus seems to lend itself particularly well to a cyclic rather than a linear approach. By this I mean that, given as an objective the capacity to express a number of concepts and functions, a course is designed to expand progressively the learner's semantic repertoire. At the lowest level he can express them only in the simplest and least differentiated manner. By the time he reaches the most advanced levels of learning he has at his disposal a range of expression capable of communicating the same notions with far greater subtlety and nuance. The labelling of the learning units at the highest and the lowest levels may be largely the same and indeed at intermediate levels the same units continue hierarchically to provide increasing expressive range. The learner is thus recycled through units with similar denominations but with greater rhetorical range. In theory at least he could work vertically, following the same semantic theme from the lowest to the highest level. Alternatively, and in practice more plausibly, he can work through all the themes at one level before returning to the same themes at the next higher level. (In the case of *faux débutants* an obvious advantage of this kind of syllabus is that they are not compelled to work continually at the same level, whether or not their previously acquired knowledge demands it.) Where in the case of a grammatical syllabus *ordering* is a matter of the linear progression of elements to be taught from the beginning to the end of a course, in a notional syllabus the ordering is a matter of the relationship between the different cycles, there being possibly less attention paid to ordering within each phase of the cycle. (See below, p. 66).

What then is the basis of ordering in a notional syllabus? This is probably best answered by looking at the range of forms through which one function can be realized. Let us take the category of *permission* and look at the type of utterances used to *seek* permission (rather than *give* it or *deny* it). The list below has been arrived at through introspection and although it cannot possibly be said to be exhaustive (even some of the forms given can be readily recombined), it presents a wide range of utterances containing linguistic features which are habitually associated with the seeking of permission. As will be seen, the utterances are arranged in roughly ascending order of length. Forms within parenthesis are optional.

(1)   O.K.?
      All right?   } (All accompanied by an appropriate gesture,
      Any objections?   } e.g. lifting the telephone.)

(2)   Can
      May
      Could   } I use your telephone, (please)?
      Might

      Could } I { possibly } use your telephone?
      Might }   { perhaps }

(3)   Please let me use your telephone?
      Will you let me use your telephone, if I pay for the call?

(4)   Is it all right to use your telephone?

      If it's all right { with } you, I'll use your telephone?
                        { by   }

(5)   Am I allowed to use your telephone?

(6)   Do you mind if I use your telephone?
      Do you mind me using your telephone?
      Would you mind if I used your telephone?
      Would you mind me using your telephone?
      Would you mind awfully if I used your telephone?
      If you don't mind, I'll use your telephone.
      You don't mind if I use your telephone, (do you?)

      I'd like } to use your telephone. { Would } you mind?
      I want   }   { Do   }

(7)   Do you { object   } to me using your telephone?
             { have any objection }
      If you have no objection, I'll use your telephone.
      I wonder if you have any objection to me using your telephone.

(8)   Will   } you { permit } me to use your telephone?
      Would }   { allow   }
                     { consent   to me using your telephone?
                     {   { your consent   } for me to use your
                     { give   { your permission } telephone?

(9)   I (therefore) request that I be allowed to use your telephone.

(10)
                                 { let   }
      Would you be so kind as to { permit } me (to) use your
                                 { allow   }   telephone?
                                 { etc.   }

(11)

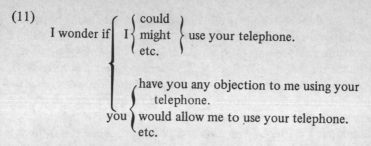

(12) Would it be possible / Is it possible } (for me) to use your telephone?

(13)

Do you think {
I could use your telephone?
you would have any objection if I used your telephone?
you would allow me to use your telephone?
it would be possible for me to use your telephone?
you could let me use your telephone?
etc.

(14) Would it be too much to ask if I could use your telephone?

(15) I don't suppose you'd be prepared to let me use your telephone, (would you?)

(16) I should be most grateful if you would permit me to use your telephone.

The very scale of variation in the forms through which permission can be sought demonstrates how impossible it would be to bring all the relevant language within a single language teaching unit labelled *seeking permission*. The learning of the forms listed above would have to be distributed over a considerable period of time. It is not difficult to see how a cyclically organized course could contain a unit *seeking permission* at each level of learning. The linguistic forms introduced at each level would be different or, to put it more accurately, at each level the learner would be taken from the forms met at the lower cycles to the forms being encountered for the first time in the new cycle. All the forms would expand the learner's repertoire of ways of seeking permission. While the function could only be performed in a limited fashion at the end of the first cycle, the learner would have at his disposal an impressive rhetorical range by the time he had completed the later cycles.

Before we could determine a suitable pedagogic sequence, we would have to discover what it is that governs the speaker's choice from among these different forms. We would find out that the options facing the speaker were principally stylistic, though the setting and the speaker's own presuppositions would also be relevant. Of particular importance are the stylistic dimensions of *interpersonal relations* and *medium* (speech or writing). The dimension of interpersonal relations requires that the form of an utterance should be appropriate to one's relationship with the person addressed. The expression of this relationship is a matter of *formality* and *politeness.* While it is difficult to be categorical about degrees of formality, we can probably distinguish three levels in the suggested utterances. These are *casual* (least formal), *consultative* (neutral) and *formal* (most formal). According to such a classification the utterances of (1) would be regarded as casual, (8), (9) and (16) would be formal and the remainder would be consultative. As for politeness, all of the forms listed above would be acceptable in the right context. The minimal utterances of (1) would cause no offence if the speaker was in the office of a friend at the time. If the speaker was a person that one had only just met for the first time, they would probably be reguarded as less acceptable. Coming from somebody to whom one has just opened one's front door, they would be taken as decidely discourteous. The consultative forms vary in their degree of politeness. In general the more tentative forms (as indicated by the use of past tenses, conditionals, the embedding of the principal content in a subordinate clause etc.), are usually considered the more polite. It seems to be thought less demanding to express a need in an indirect way. The more the speaker needs to suggest that the person he is addressing is doing him a favour by conceding his request for permission, the more likely he is to use a form marked for politeness. The less well he knows the person he is speaking to, the less likely it is that he will choose a form that seems to anticipate the outcome of his request. Just as one can deliberately (or inadvertently) offend by choosing a form unmarked for politeness in a setting where a marked form would be expected, one can achieve the same effect in a situation where a marked form is not needed by opting for a heavily marked form like that of (14) or (15). The effect could be compounded by choice of an appropriate intonation contour.

While any of the forms cited *could* appear in speech, a number of them would be impossible in writing. The utterances of (1) would simply not be understood; those of (2) are scarcely acceptable as they stand, but become more so if they are embedded in a context such as 'I am writing to ask whether . . . (I can use your caravan etc.).' The formal utterances are much more readily provided with a written than with a spoken context. This is hardly surprising since writing is less often informal and when it is, perhaps it is not often used to seek permission. By the same token even at the same level of formality the more polite forms are likely to be preferred.

The reason why the written forms tend to be more formal and more polite is that less information is provided by the setting in which the act of communication is taking place. Whatever is to be conveyed must, therefore, be explicitly marked. The setting is important in a number of ways. The utterances of (1) can only be understood if they are accompanied by the right gestures and facial expressions and if there is a telephone actually present in the physical environment. As realizations of the function *seeking permission* they are, therefore, very much context-bound. They would be largely useless if the permission sought related to a situation other than that in which the language event is taking place or, indeed, if the permission did not relate to physical acts or entities at all. In either of these cases they could not be self-sufficient as requests for permission, although they could be part of a larger linguistic sequence having the same overall function. A man may ask his boss for a day's holiday in the following way:

I'm thinking of taking next Monday off. Any objections?

It is the utterance as a whole that has the function of seeking permission, not just the phrase *any objections?* which is quite inexplicit by itself. The setting may prove very significant from the teaching point of view because the regular occurrence of a function in a specific setting may lead to one particular form becoming associated with that setting. A schoolchild who wants to leave his or her class to go to the lavatory in British English at least, conventionally asks:

Can I be excused, please?

and not, for example,

Would you be so kind as to permit me to be excused.

In many situations, especially where economy is much appreciated, the more polite forms would be regarded as pedantic and time-wasting. A traveller who presented himself at a railway ticket office with a large queue behind him would arouse nothing but opprobrium if he said:

I wonder whether you would be so kind as to let me have a second-class return to Waterloo.

Permission to do something is rarely sought under quite such pressing circumstances, but what is important is the general point that language functions may well be realized in conventional ways according to the situation.

These examples given relate only to the borrowing of somebody's telephone, and this is hardly asking for a major favour. Nor would the outcome of the request normally be much in doubt. Nonetheless the difference in the forms is to some extent also a difference in the expectations of the speaker. Someone who has said:

You don't mind if I use your telephone, do you?

would presumably be rather surprised if the answer was *Yes!*
On the other hand *I don't suppose you'd be prepared to lend me your Rolls, would you?* with the appropriate intonation, seems to anticipate a negative answer. Of course, the speaker may use such a negatively oriented form even though he does anticipate that permission will be given. He does so in order to give the impression of presuming the least upon the other person's goodwill. Most of the listed forms do not have either a positive or a negative marking. (5) above is distinct in that it addresses itself to the permissibility of the act whether or not this is within the control of the person addressed. Depending on what kind of permission it is that is being sought, the addressee will either report whether the proposed act is permitted or will himself grant that permission (or not, as the case may be). As before, the speaker may represent as an objective issue something that is in fact within the power of the interlocutor.

Having noted the features that help to determine the precise form selected by a speaker, we can begin to see how a process of limitation and ordering might operate. The starting-point for syllabus design is a semantic and behavioural prediction, which sets up the overall objectives and perhaps establishes different priorities within those objectives. Such a prediction will answer the question of whether the spoken or the written language is the objective, or, if both, which has the higher priority. It will tell us whether there are specific settings (situations) of language use for which the learner is to be prepared. We can ask ourselves what kinds of interpersonal relations can be anticipated and what these imply for the degrees of formality and politeness that the learner will have to be able to express. Since we are, for the moment, discussing *global* course design, we must expect that no precise answers to such questions will be forthcoming. This does not mean that the syllabus designer cannot set objectives in these terms. It merely means that what the syllabus provides has to encompass a wider range of possible uses of language than would be necessary in a situation where accurate prediction of the learners' future language needs is possible. Given the difficulty of detailed prediction, it is likely that relatively unmarked forms of language will be given the higher priority. By this I mean that forms for asking permission which are marked for positive or negative expectations, or forms which are markedly polite or which risk being interpreted as impolite will probably be deferred until the later stages of learning.

Even when these questions have been settled, the syllabus or course designer will still find himself with considerable freedom of choice. It is here that the kind of criteria that underlie a grammatical syllabus (see page 6) can once again be turned to. Other things being equal there is no reason why we should not consider the relative pro‹ ductivity, simplicity and contrastive difficulty of the different grammatical forms before deciding the contents of the successive cycles. We might choose to introduce *seeking permission* in the first cycle in the forms *can/could I use your telephone, please*. We would judge these intuitively to be relatively simple in structure while at the same time they introduce both a major class of English verbs, the modals, and the 'modal' use of past tense forms to express tentativeness. They contrast with forms containing multiple embeddings, like *I wonder whether you would be so kind as to allow me to use your telephone*. On grammatical grounds, at least, one would presumably hesitate to include such an utterance in an early cycle. On the other hand, *would it be possible for me to use your telephone* could be learned early if it proved comparable to a mother-tongue construction.

The problem that faces the syllabus constructor is to decide just how much weighting to give to grammatical criteria. Does he first decide which forms are stylistically and situationally acceptable and then order these along the lines suggested above, or does he pay greater attention to grammatical factors and allow these on occasions to lead him to introduce forms that are not really entirely appropriate from a stylistic or sociolinguistic point of view, but which are comprehensible and do have certain grammatical advantages? If the first course is adopted the learner will certainly be faced from time to time with forms that are unusually complex for the early stages of language learning; if the latter, the learner will be led to use forms in a way that the native speaker finds inappropriate. It is within our power to omit 'permission seeking' forms from early teaching altogether. We could leave the request for permission to be inferred from the speaker's expression of his intentions — *I want to smoke, I want to use your telephone etc.* — and such permission might well be offered, although with a judgement being passed about the character of the speaker at the same time. This kind of inappropriateness is often the result of learning from a grammatical syllabus. There seems to be no reason why, in principle, this issue should be resolved one way or the other. A syllabus can still be regarded as semantic in orientation whatever the relative roles the constructor assigns to grammatical and stylistic factors. We can note here simply that it is an issue that has to be faced in constructing a notional syllabus and that there is no justification for insisting upon one particular solution. The syllabus designer has to settle the matter to his own satisfaction.

The foregoing discussion relates to the question of ordering in so far as this is a matter of moving from one cycle to the next higher cycle while remaining within units of similar denomination. When we consider units within the same cycle, that is to say, the linear sequence of units with different denominations, it is not clear that there is any intrinsic ordering to the categories we have introduced. It is not clear either that there is any intrinsic way of *linking* one unit to the next. One of the difficulties to be faced by anyone designing a course on notional principles, therefore, is how to overcome undue fragmentation of the units at any one level. A series of linguistically and thematically unconnected units may appear lacking in coherence to the learner, especially in the case of low-intensity courses. As in existing courses this coherence might be provided by the introduction of a story line. This would have the effect of ensuring thematic continuity and of helping to resolve questions of the ordering of the categories in relation to one another. It is a solution, however, which is extrinsic to the idea of the notional syllabus itself.

Although we are at this point discussing notional syllabuses in general, the issues have been illustrated by reference to a *functionally* defined learning unit. Things do not look quite the same if we turn to the *conceptual* (semantico-grammatical) part of the notional framework. (There is no explicit discussion here of the *modal* content, parts of which resemble the functional and parts of which resemble the notional content.) We have already seen that the expression of ideational meaning is closely associated with control of the grammatical categories of the language. Form and meaning are not, however, in a one-to-one relation. Many prepositions express spatial, temporal and purely grammatical relations. Even within spatial reference, the same preposition may be used for more than one spatial concept and the same concept may be expressed through different prepositions. Past acts are not referred to solely through use of the past tense, nor is the past tense used only for this purpose. There is, therefore, a lack of congruence between grammatical and semantic systems. It is taken here to be almost axiomatic that the acquisition of the grammatical system of a language remains a most important element in language learning. The grammar is the means through which linguistic creativity is ultimately achieved and an inadequate knowledge of the grammar would lead to a serious limitation on the capacity for communication. A notional syllabus, no less than a grammatical syllabus, must seek to ensure that the grammatical system is properly assimilated by the learner. We do not express language functions in isolation. We do not simply *order;* we order someone *to do something.* We do not simply *deny;* we deny *something.* We do not *explain;* we explain *something.* The *something* (here the *conceptual meaning*) is what the grammar of the language in conjunction with the lexicon expresses. What we can express through language still depends on, among other things, how far we have mastered the grammatical rules that underlie the production of utterances.

If we accept that the grammar is this important, we must decide how we can most effectively plan for its acquisition in the case of global courses having a generally semantic orientation. Do we approach the conceptual content in the same way as we have suggested the functional content might be approached? That is to say, do we, to put it somewhat simplistically, isolate particular categories of meaning, determine the different forms through which these can be realized and then order these in some way in the syllabus? If we attempt to do it this way, we will be sure to meet certain problems. For a start it will be much more difficult to manipulate the conceptual content of sentences than the functional content. In any sentence several aspects of conceptual meaning are present simultaneously. It is therefore very difficult to isolate one kind of meaning. The decision to deal with 'Time when' will first lead us to certain prepositions which are used in the relevant expressions: *at, on, in.* We will then have to decide whether the point of time is to be located in the past, present or future (if not something more complex). This in turn will require decisions about verb forms. A decision will then be needed on *what* it is that is taking place at the given point of time. This will lead in turn to one or more kinds of relational meaning and almost certainly to deictic meaning too. The use of any noun introduces quantitative meaning. It is unlikely, therefore, that categories of meaning can be introduced with much rigour.

It is furthermore difficult to keep tabs on the grammatical categories themselves when a semantic category involves widely differing parts of the grammatical system. Let us suppose we wished to include units on the making of *generic* statements. In English this would require us to deal at some point with such things as: the appropriate verb forms, (principally, but not only, the present tense), the use of articles, grammatical number, frequency adverbs and frequency adverbials, the distinction between stative and dynamic adjectives. These are obviously widely diverse, but they are also all categories that would have to be handled elsewhere under other semantic headings. The respective grammatical categories are not covered exhaustively when they have made an appearance in one, semantically defined unit.

I do not wish to suggest that it is in principle impossible to plan the conceptual content of language syllabuses in this way. However, it does seem to me clear that it would in practice prove to be an extremely complex task; the more so if we are simultaneously trying to introduce language functions which have been contextualized in suitable situations.

While not rejecting the possibility that such an approach might ultimately prove practicable, I would suggest that there are alternative procedures which can much more easily be followed without losing sight of the generally notional approach proposed here. The weakest application would involve use of only the functional (and modal) part of the notional framework. That is to say, an overall syllabus could be conventionally grammatical in its early stages and would become semantic, i.e. functional, only in its later stages. To put it another way, the functional categories could be used to provide a linguistic rationale for the post-intermediate stages of language learning, while the earlier stages retain their present form. It would be more accurate to call such a syllabus (the second part, that is) *functional* than *notional*.

The stronger alternative, while admitting that the grammatical facts of language require that grammatically motivated decisions will sometimes have to be taken, places far more weight on semantic criteria in the selecting and ordering of grammatical forms than is normal in a grammatical syllabus. It does not, however, go so far as to propose that the grammatical content should be derived from a prior semantic specification. One might set out, therefore, to present systematically the verbal system of English as most courses do, but the ordering of the forms might differ from that conventionally followed because we wish to give the learner, early on in his learning, the capacity to distinguish past, present and future time. Indeed, in a strictly grammatical approach the absence of a specific future tense in the English verbal system often leads to future reference being introduced only later in a course because it is the secondary use of forms which have some other principal meaning. (The fact that some courses still have units devoted to the 'future tense' in English indicates both the continuing influence of Latinate grammar and the fact that even grammatical syllabuses are often affected by semantic considerations whether or not these are explicitly acknowledged.) In such an approach there might be a unit devoted to a grammatical category such as *transitive sentences,* but we would use our semantic insight to ensure that in the first instance at least the grammatical *subjects* were all *agents* and not, say, *instruments* or *benefactives.* To take another example, we would not set up a unit simply devoted to *prepositions,* but would clearly distinguish their spatial, temporal and grammatical uses. By adding to the existing criteria for structuring the grammatical content of learning a new criterion which could be called the criterion of *semantic value* and by giving it high priority in relation, say, to the criterion of *simplicity,* we can keep within the basic philosophy of the notional approach, while making the task of controlling the grammatical content of learning rather easier. At the same time we will ensure that the grammar of the language is systematically acquired.

2.2. Special course design

The discussion of global course design has enabled us to consider some of the general issues involved in the application of notional syllabuses. However it is doubtful whether global courses provide the most effective field of application of the notional approach. In the first place the needs of the learners are in practice difficult to define; secondly, for most of the learners the opportunity actually to use the language may be long deferred. Indeed in some cases it may never come at all. Leaving the question of the learner's motivation aside, it is difficult to argue that language needs to be associated with actual communication from the beginning of the learning process.

It is a mistake, however, to assume that languages are taught only in schools or that school language learning is necessarily typical of other foreign language learning situations. The fact is that a great deal of language learning goes on elsewhere and under conditions that can be markedly in contrast with those found in school systems. It is in these situations that the notional syllabus has most to offer. What they mostly have in common is that the learner's language needs can be anticipated with a fair degree of accuracy.

2.2.1. High surrender value courses

The concept of *high surrender value* courses is a familiar one.[2] Insurance policies may offer the policy-holder large terminal benefits, but if he is obliged to surrender his policy for cash before it reaches its term, the sum he receives may be considerably less than would be expected from the amount already invested. However, there are other kinds of policy which deliberately take into account the possibility of early surrender. For the same investment they offer a smaller terminal benefit, but a higher sum is received in the event of premature surrender of the policy. Global courses are generally like the first kind of policy. They are regarded as an investment for the future. There

---

[2] A term I was introduced to by Professor S.P. Corder.

are, however, other learners who may need to cash their investment immediately. Whatever they learn may be needed immediately for the purpose of communication. They cannot afford to be told that in due course they will be able to make use of what they are learning. (It may be, of course, that global courses should meet the same conditions, but that is not the issue here.)

In cases like this it can be argued that it is not enough simply to apply an additional semantic criterion to an existing grammatical basis for syllabus design. Instead, both the functional and the conceptual content of learning needs to be planned from the beginning so that what is likely to be most urgently needed for communication is what is actually taught first. The syllabus designer emphasizes first those concepts and functions which will need to be expressed in even the most limited types of interaction. Rudimentary distinctions of time, place and relational meaning, together with some commonly occurring language functions, such as greetings, requests and apologies, might well occupy the early stages of learning, whether or not they also introduce grammatical productive items.

The need for 'continuous application' courses is most likely to be found in the field of adult language learning. It would be felt particularly strongly by people who are newly resident, perhaps as immigrants or 'guest workers', in a country whose language they do not speak. While the language for essential social and work functions has to be learned immediately, in the longer term a much more widely based proficiency is required if the individual is to gain integration into and acceptance by the host community. By means of a notional syllabus both the short- and the long-term objectives can be met. Much the same can be said if the learner is not a resident but is, or expects to be, a regular visitor to the country concerned. Many adult language learners fall into this category.

It can be argued that the social functions of language do not need to be taught since these are the very things that tend to be picked up by someone who is regularly in contact with native speakers. While there is an element of truth in this, it ignores the fact that it is possible to survive in a community with only the most rudimentary knowledge of the language. Communication that is adequate for survival, though no more, can take place by use of a handful of essential lexical items supplemented by gestures. It is common for foreign residents to reach a plateau in their skill in a language and for that plateau itself to be at a very low level. A notional syllabus would not stop short at preparing learners for unavoidable social interactions; it would seek to prepare the learner for those kinds of communication which the learner *can*, if he chooses, avoid, but which it is not in his longer-term interest to avoid. It is true, however, that the initial emphasis would be on the most urgently required uses of language.

2.2.2. Limited duration courses

Limited duration courses have a good deal in common with continuous application courses, the principal difference being that in the latter no limit is set on the ultimate objectives of the learner, whereas in the former a limit is set by the amount of time at the learner's disposal. (It should perhaps be said that actual language courses may well be regarded by some learners as complete in themselves, but by others as a basis for further learning. I would argue that a notional syllabus is particularly appropriate in such circumstances since it can meet defined communication needs while at the same time it is constructing a more widely based linguistic competence.)

Although it must be admitted that a proportion of language learners are always uncertain as to their purposes in learning a language, a more reliable prediction of future language needs can usually be made than is the case with global language courses. The essential task in planning such courses, therefore, is to reconcile the needs to the time available for learning. With a grammatical syllabus one can do little more than teach whatever percentage of some ultimate grammatical specification is permitted by the time available. The resulting competence may well not provide a communicative repertoire that is in any way relevant to the learner's needs. A notional approach ensures that what is learned has maximum communicative value.

When we speak of limited duration courses, we may mean courses lasting 10, 50, 100 or 200 hours. Given such widely different conditions, it is inevitable and right that there should be great variation in the types of course provided. Indeed this should be one of the specific virtues of the notional syllabus. Considering the varying amounts of time available leads us to some interesting observations about the nature of differing levels of communicative competence that can be achieved in a notional approach.

For example, what do we do for a business-man who tells us that in two weeks' time he is going to Japan for the first time and that he can spare about ten hours to learn a little Japanese? What would we do if he said that he had fifty hours available? We can perhaps begin to find the answer to such questions by considering what we noted when we looked at the many ways in which someone can seek permission. (See pp. 59-60.) We saw that the minimal utterances that can perform these functions are utterances which are quite inexplicit in their form, but

whose function can be readily inferred from the context. The
language was 'context-bound' in the sense that it would not be meaningful outside the context of utterance. The solution to the problem
of the ten-hour course may be not to attempt to teach any of the
grammar of the language but to provide him with a strategy for
'context-bound' communication. Bearing in mind that the very fact
that he is a stranger, and visibly so, is part of the contextual information
available to the person he addresses, he can be taught a strategy for
communication, probably consisting largely of forms of address
(greetings, gratitude) essential lexical items (perhaps with, for example,
interrogative words added), and intonation and paralinguistic features
(for example, gestures and facial expressions). To these would have to
be added some cultural do's and don't's. The learner will produce
forms of language which, in normal circumstances, would be quite un-
acceptable and even formally incorrect, but what he knows will be
wholly useful to him and it is doubtful whether this would be the case
if those ten hours were devoted to a rapid run through the grammar of
Japanese.

The fifty-hour course would presumably require a different
solution. We can admit a more ambitious objective than the pidgin-like
knowledge of the language that the ten-hour course would produce.
On the other hand fifty hours is not sufficient contact for a thorough
knowledge of the language to be built up. The objective here might be
to separate the learner from his dependence on context for communication. This means that he must learn to express the selected concepts
and functions in a way that is grammatically largely acceptable. We
could not conceivably expect to teach the whole of the grammar in
this time. It would be a specifically reduced grammar that was learned.
Because it is potentially more productive this approach seems superior
to teaching a large number of useful formulae rather as one might
learn from a phrase-book. On the other hand we would have to admit
that there was probably insufficient time to ensure that the forms
learned are inevitably sociolinguistically or stylistically appropriate.
Our fifty-hour learner, needing to find his way to the station, might
be able to say simply, 'Where is the station?', but not, 'I wonder if you
could tell me the way to the station?' We might, therefore define our
objectives at the fifty-hour level as being to produce the ability to
express an important set of functions in grammatically acceptable but
not necessarily stylistically appropriate ways. It would be the task of
the one and two hundred hour courses to ensure both grammatical
and stylistic acceptability.

2.2.3. Learning language for special purposes

Special purpose language courses are those in which the learners' objectives are unusually well defined. Very commonly they are professional language courses in the sense that the learner needs the language for the more efficient exercise of his occupation. There may be considerable limitation in the language skills needed (reading, writing, speaking and listening) and in the topics the learner will need to be able to handle and the functions he will have to perform.

It is recognized that what the learner needs in these circumstances is often a restricted kind of language, in that the vocabulary has a rather specialized character and the grammar is either somewhat limited in its range or has unusual distribution. Forms that occur in conversational language may be wholly absent from one specialized use of language but may occur with abnormally high frequency in another. This has led people to propose the concept of *varieties of language* (registers). What lawyers use is said to be *legal English.* Engineers use *engineering English,* doctors *medical English* and business-men *business English.* They are varieties of English which are related to but are not identical with what we might, without further definition, call *common-core English.* If our approach to the design of language syllabuses is a synthetic one, the task of providing the learner with the language skill he needs is seen as a matter of teaching him the different constituents of the specialized lexicon and the skewed grammar. We are basing ourselves on a grammatical syllabus, but the grammar involved is not identical with that which is taught in global language courses.

If we adopt a notional approach, we do not deny these linguistic facts but we do regard them in a rather different light. In the first place a more behaviourally oriented analysis of their needs may reveal that simply to identify the needs of doctors with something called *medical English* or *medical German* is quite inadequate. We might take medical English to be best represented by the language found in medical textbooks (though the differences between medical textbooks might be just as significant as the similarities). But then our putative learner may need the language for purposes other than the reading of medical textbooks. Will he also want to read articles reporting current research? Will he want to look at more popular articles on medical advances? Will he need to read about the administration of his profession? Will he be dealing with patients in the language? Will he be communicating with medical and administrative colleagues? If so, will this be in writing or in speech, or, indeed, both? It can be seen that analysing needs in such behavioural terms is far more enlightening

about what the individual will have to learn than simply dealing in
terms of a somewhat gross concept like *medical English.*

Although, then, actual language needs are likely to be more
complex than simply to be able to operate a particular variety of
language, the fact remains that specific texts may have characteristic
linguistic features and a knowledge of these features may be at least
part of what the learner has to acquire. If we simply make a grammatical inventory of these features (ignoring here the lexical features
which need little explanation), we are failing to offer any information
as to why particular texts have the specific features that characterize
them. If we look at it from a semantic point of view, we can see why
it is that texts in different domains may be grammatically distinguish-
able from one another. Different types of text are written with
different purposes in mind and, indeed, even within one text, the
intention will vary from one part to another. Our medical textbooks
will presumably contain anatomical *descriptions;* hence, they will
employ language forms appropriate to description. They will contain
definitions; in consequence, the linguistic forms for making definitions will be found in such texts. They will need to make *generic*
statements; therefore, generic grammatical forms will be a recurrent
feature. There will be surgical or other *instructions;* as a result, the
language forms related to the giving of instructions will be found. The
four terms italicized above are semantic, not grammatical. The fact
that the texts have certain grammatical features follows from the fact
that the texts are written with different purposes.

Basing the provision of special language courses on a notional
syllabus means taking advantage both of this insight and of the
greater accuracy in the prediction of needs that is provided by a
more behaviourally oriented analysis. The insight about the relation
of the grammar to the writer's intention is pedagogically significant
because it means that the learning of the grammatical features of
specialized texts is not the acquisition of a somewhat random
inventory of items, but can be organized on functional lines. The
learner is shown how to describe, how to instruct, how to define
and so on. This is altogether more meaningful than learning intensive
clauses, impersonal passives, the present tense and so on, although the
results in purely grammatical terms may be the same. It is likely that
the teaching of special language courses will be largely based on the
use of authentic texts (see also below p.78). The semantic dimension
will enter the teaching, not as a result of prior semantic selection, as
has been suggested in the case of other courses, but in the way in
which the texts are exploited.

2.2.4. Remedial courses

The courses discussed so far have all been by implication *ab initio* courses (or, in the case of the last section, the specialization of existing knowledge). A remedial course is different in that learning of the language has taken place previously, but the resulting competence is inadequate as a consequence either of forgetting or of unsatisfactory teaching and learning. There is no point in a separate discussion of the construction of syllabuses for remedial courses since the principles are no different from those that have already been discussed. Specific mention is made here of such courses only because a semantic orientation seems to offer particular advantages in this case.

The remedial learner is characterized by the fact that his knowledge of the language is uneven and relatively unpredictable. With a grammatical syllabus the strategy adopted is to cover again the ground that was covered in the learner's previous courses and, when the gaps have been filled, to continue to higher levels with the same synthetic mode of teaching. The disadvantages of this are that it involves a good deal of repetition that is, in practice, unnecessary, that teaching the same kind of material by the same kinds of methods is hardly going to impress on the learner that he is making much progress in his learning and, finally, that the very fact that the learner is following a remedial course at all means that he did not learn satisfactorily from the kinds of teaching that he received previously and that therefore some different approach is needed. (It is only fair to admit that there are learners who cling closely to what is familiar and who might resist novelty in a remedial course.) What a notional, and particularly a functional syllabus offers is the possibility of acquiring new and relevant types of language competence while, at the same time, weaknesses in purely grammatical competence can be dealt with as they arise. Of course, if and when the initial language teaching has been based on a notional syllabus, some of this advantage will be lost, but one cannot foresee this being the case in the near future.

2.3. Lexical content

The principal concern in this discussion of syllabus design has been to discover the most effective ways in which the functional and grammatical aspects of linguistic competence can be developed. The learning of lexical items has been mentioned only incidentally. As we saw in the first chapter, in a grammatical syllabus the lexical content is determined according to a variety of criteria of which frequency is perhaps the most important. In a notional syllabus, while concepts of frequency are not irrelevant, there are other sources from which vocabulary will in the first place be derived.

To a certain, though limited, extent the semantico-grammatical categories themselves have implications for the lexical content. Concepts of time, quantity and space cannot be expressed without an appropriate lexicon. Communicating emotional reactions too may involve drawing on a certain set of lexical items. In general, however, the categories of communicative function do not so much demand a specific lexical content as operate on a lexicon determined by other factors.

One of these factors will be the situation of language use. We saw above that a function is only realized in a specific context and indeed would only be taught in a specific context. That context may well be a *situational* context and, in that case, the lexical content taught will be that which is appropriate to the situation. Any prior analysis of needs has to take anticipated situations of language use into account and in doing so it goes part of the way towards defining the lexical content of learning. The context, however, may be *linguistic* as much as situational and, in this case, the exact form of an utterance will be dependent on the general semantic orientation of the text in which it occurs. Words can be drawn up into semantically related sets. To put it another way, the lexical content of utterances is often a matter of the *topics* being talked about. If the topic is itself associated with the physical setting, the lexical need has already been predicted from the situational analysis; but, more often than not, there is no particular relationship between the setting in which language is produced and the topic which is being talked or written about.

The lexical content of learning, therefore, can be largely derived from an analysis of the topics likely to occur in the language use of a given group. In the case of specialized language learners the topics obviously derive from the field of specialization; in the case of non-specialized learners it is probably necessary to establish a number of themes around which semantically related items can be grouped and from which in constructing a notional syllabus an appropriate selection can be made. Such an approach to specifying the lexical content is obviously very much in keeping with the general philosophy of the notional syllabus with its emphasis on the content and purpose of language communication.

To give an idea of what is meant here by *topic*, it might be worth-while giving an example. The topics below have been used in the specification of learning content for beginners in the context of adult

language learning:[3]
    Personal identification
    House and home
    Trade, profession, occupation
    Free time, entertainment
    Travel
    Relations with other people
    Health and welfare
    Education
    Shopping
    Food and drink
    Services
    Places
    Foreign language
    Weather
This list was produced for use in a given context. It is not exhaustive, nor would it necessarily be appropriate in other contexts.

3.0. Some implications for the process of teaching

This book is not primarily concerned with either the materials or the techniques which are to be used in putting a notional syllabus into effect. However, although, strictly speaking, questions of the linguistic basis of courses (i.e. the syllabus) are distinct from questions of methodology, it is hardly likely that one can revise so radically one's view of the full nature of the linguistic behaviour aimed at, without there being implications for the more detailed aspects of the teaching process. Both in teaching and in evaluating our students, we need to adopt procedures that are congruent with what we regard as the proper objectives of language teaching. In proposing that the semantic dimension should be given the highest priority in syllabus design, we are implying that the success of our teaching should be judged by whether or not our pupils are able to communicate meanings appropriately. To ensure that this is so, we need to introduce new forms of language learning materials and we need to have at our disposal new techniques of assessment.

---

[3] J.A. van Ek: The Threshold Level. Strasbourg. Council of Europe. 1975.

3.1. Teaching materials

It would be premature to suggest that we are already in a position to put forward a coherent and adequate account of the methods and techniques to be used with a notional syllabus. However, the model of communication that underlies the notional approach suggests that certain kinds of material will be more prominent than is usually the case. In the model we have a *producer* and a *receiver*, but we also have positive interaction between the two in the sense that the receiver in turn becomes a producer. The discussion so far has centred almost exclusively on the producer of language. We have talked largely in terms of what the learner should be able to communicate in or do through the language. This reflects the fact that it is normal as the principal objective in language teaching to regard the creation of a productive repertoire in the learner. The notional approach has been used so far only to re-define the nature of this repertoire. If, however, we focus first on the receiver and then on the process of interaction, we shall see that our model implies more radical changes in the teaching of languages than would be necessary simply to 'semanticize' existing forms of exercise or drill. The needs of the receiver will lead us to consideration of the place of *authentic language materials;* the interactional nature of much communication will lead us to emphasize the place of *role-playing.*

3.1.1. The use of authentic materials

By talking so far principally in terms of the predicted content and purpose of the learner's own utterances, we have concentrated on the learner as a potential *producer* of language. However, any discussion of verbal interaction implies comprehension as well as production of language, and it would therefore be wrong to give the impression that syllabus planning is planning for production only. By focussing on the receiver we are obliged to consider the content and purpose, not only of the utterances he may produce, but of those he may hear or read.

In a context where we are emphasizing the communicative purpose of language and the immediate usefulness of the language being learned, the acquisition of comprehension skill poses a particular problem. Whereas the individual is the master of what he himself chooses to say, he can exercise no comparable control over the language he hears. If the language is to be encountered only in the classroom, this presents no great difficulty, since the teacher can control both the language that the pupil produces and the language that he hears. Conventionally this control is exercised in such a way that the pupil hears diverse and complex language forms only in the later stages of learning. However, the essence of the semantic approach is that we do envisage the possibility of immediate language use. This in turn means that the learner will have to try to understand far more varied forms of language than he is capable of producing himself. We cannot normally afford to give the learner a receptive repertoire that is as limited as his productive repertoire will be.

In some ways this is merely a new form of a familiar issue. Learners who have followed conventional language courses and who may have developed a considerable classroom competence find that when they come into contact with native speakers of the language, they meet serious problems in comprehension. They may be able to perform adequately themselves in speech, but they frequently cannot understand what native speakers say to them. The fact is that they are not accustomed to hearing (or reading) the language as it is produced *by* native speakers *for* native speakers.

This suggests that in language courses generally, but in courses based on a notional syllabus in particular, much more attention needs to be paid to the acquisition of a receptive competence and that an important feature of materials designed to produce such a competence would be authentic language materials. By this is meant materials which have not been specially written or recorded for the foreign learner, but which were originally directed at a native-speaking audience. Such materials need not even be edited, in the sense that linguistically difficult sections would not be deleted, although the linguistic content of such texts could well be exploited in various ways. The importance of incorporating such materials into courses is that they will provide the only opportunity that the learner will have to see the contrast between the somewhat idealized language that he is acquiring and the apparently deficient forms that people actually use, to meet the forms of language current in speech and to develop the ability to understand language that he will never need to produce. In short, such materials will be the means by which he can bridge the gap between classroom knowledge and an effective capacity to participate in real language events.

It is, of course, a good deal easier to provide authentic *written* materials than authentic *spoken* materials. Indeed, in many countries there is a tradition of the study of unsimplified literary texts at a post-intermediate level of language learning. This partly explains why most learners have always been more advanced in reading comprehension than in other language skills. We would, no doubt, wish to extend their contact with authentic written materials to include non-literary texts, but this is relatively easily done. Authentic spoken materials, however, can only be presented to learners if the necessary technological support is available. Tape-recorders are already widely in use and some materials containing authentic listening texts do exist. Useful as these are, they lack the visual element that is often a feature of spoken language situations and which provides the learner with valuable support in the form of clear contextualization and the presence of many paralinguistic features which help to make the language meaningful. As television and video-cassettes become a more established part of the resources available for language learning, we can expect that semantically oriented courses will introduce learners to authentic materials from the beginning and that this contact will not be deferred until the learner has supposedly mastered all the forms that he or she is likely to hear. In this way we shall be able to avoid the dilemma of the user of a phrase-book, who is able to ask the way, but is then unable to understand the answer.

3.1.2.   Role-playing

In a synthetic approach to language teaching the principal objective is usually seen as the creation of a mastery of sentence construction. The preoccupation is with intra-sentential grammatical relations and the meanings which grammatical forms express. In general, therefore, the sentence as a unit of teaching is regarded as an adequate vehicle for the presentation of what has to be learned. It provides an adequate context for the display of the grammatical forms that are being taught. In certain methods, notably the audio-lingual method, the sentence may be embedded in a dialogue, but the dialogue, though providing a context, does not necessarily clarify the meaning of the individual sentences in any way.

In our discussion of the linguistic facts underlying a notional syllabus we noticed, first, that the function of an individual utterance is often not deducible from its form, but can only be discovered when the context in which it occurs is fully taken into account and, secondly, that there are recurrent, though not fixed, patterns of interaction through language so that different language functions may chain together in not unpredictable ways. These facts suggest that in contrast to the sentence-level learning of a synthetic approach, learning based on a notional syllabus demands a linguistic context for utterances that is larger than the sentence and might well be founded on the typical sequences of language functions that recur in natural language use.

It would seem to follow that the use of dialogues in teaching is far more crucial than is the case in synthetic approaches, that such dialogues should be based much more closely on the kinds of linguistic interaction that take place in real language use and should not be treated simply as ways of contextualising particular grammatical structures, and that the contribution of the learner should be to play those roles in the dialogues that we can predict he will take subsequently in real acts of communication. We can foresee therefore that role-playing is likely to be a most important technique in teaching to a notional, and particularly a functional, syllabus. It will ensure that all utterances are properly contextualised and it will require the learner to attempt to exhibit the very language behaviour that we have defined as the principal objective of language learning.

3.2. Testing

We end by posing a problem rather than by offering a solution. In adopting a notional syllabus we have defined both the larger and the more specific objectives in new terms. This reflects a more complete view of the nature of language. It should perhaps be self-evident that the process of evaluation in language teaching is closely related to objectives. We test a learner's language skill in order both to establish what he knows (or what he can do) and to assess how successful we have been in our teaching in adding to his linguistic achievement. If we see language learning as primarily the acquisition of a mastery of grammatical structure, the emphasis of our tests will also be on the grammar of the language. If we regard a command of the phonological contrasts as important, this fact too will be reflected in the form of our tests. Where teaching is, in our terms, synthetic, testing will tend to be so too. That is to say, in testing as in teaching, the language is broken down into what are regarded as its component parts.

While I would in no way wish to suggest that the information gathered by such forms of evaluation is not valuable, it is, I think, clear that it is not sufficient in the light of the view taken here of the true objectives of language learning. Performance on such tests is not necessarily an accurate guide to what we might call the individual's 'capacity to communicate'. We take this capacity to be the ability to encode a message correctly, certainly, but also spontaneously, fluently and appropriately. It is normally correctness that is tested and not these other features of actual language performance, but we should bear in mind that we have in a way extended the notion of correctness here to include not only the capacity to construct grammatically (and phonologically) well-formed sentences, but the capacity to select these forms in order to express many different kinds of conceptual, modal and functional meaning. This is something that we have scarcely begun to assess in a systematic way in language testing.

The tests involved would inevitably be largely tests of integrated rather than isolated skills. They would also be tests of language performance. The problem of testing actual performance are well-known. In the context of a notional syllabus it means that we will be seeking the answer to the question of whether the learner can express such things as concepts of time, spatial relationships, possibilities, intentions, promises, forgiveness, prohibitions, affirmations, conjectures, surprise, solicitude — indeed any of the sub-categories that are proposed for the notional syllabus. (In practice, of course, far more narrowly defined than here.) At the moment, I think it is true to say that we do not know how to obtain the answers to such questions. We do not know how to establish the communicative proficiency of the learner. It should not be inferred from this that a notional syllabus cannot operate until the problem of testing is resolved. It would be a strange set of priorities that limited a teaching programme to what we were able to test effectively. But the forms of testing do have a considerable influence on the manner and the content of language teaching and it is important that while some people are experimenting with the notional syllabus as such, others should be attempting to develop the new testing techniques that should, ideally, accompany it. Indeed, such techniques would be a valuable contribution to language testing whether or not the proposals here for a notional syllabus come to be widely accepted.

BIBLIOGRAPHY

Allen, R.L., *The Verb System of Present-Day American English*. The Hague, Mouton, 1966.

Alston, W.P., Meaning and use. In Parkinson (ed.) 1968.

Austin, J.L., *How To Do Things With Words*. Oxford, Clarendon Press, 1962.

Bongers, H., *The History and Principles of Vocabulary Control*. Wocopi, Woerden, 1947.

Bright, J.A. and G.P. McGregor, *Teaching English as a Second Language*. London, Longman, 1970.

Brunot, F., La Pensée et la Langue. Masson, Paris, 1936.

Bung, K., *The Specification of Objectives in a Language Learning System for Adults*. Strasbourg, Council of Europe, 1973.

Committee on Vocabulary Selection, *Interim Report on Vocabulary Selection*. London, King, 1936.

Dusková L. and V. Urbanová, A frequency count of English tenses with application to teaching English as a foreign language. In *Prague Studies in Mathematical Linguistics*, 2. Munich, Hueber, Prague, Academia, 1967.

van Ek, J.A., The threshold level. Strasbourg, Council of Europe, 1975.

Engels, L.K., The fallacy of word-counts. IRAL 6/3, 1968.

Fillmore, C.J., The case for case. In Bach E. and R.T. Harms (eds.) *Universals in Linguistic Theory*. New York, Holt, Rinehart, 1968.

Fries, C.C., *Teaching and Learning English as a Foreign Language*. Ann Arbor, University of Michigan, 1947.

Fries, C.C. and A.A. Traver, *English Word Lists*. Ann Arbor, University of Michigan, 1950.

George, H.V., A verb-form frequency count. ELT 18/1, 1963.

Halliday, M.A.K., Notes on transitivity and theme in English. Journal of Linguistics, 3/1, 1967.

Halliday, M.A.K., Functional diversity in language. Foundations of Language, 6, 1970.

Halliday, M.A.K., A.McIntosh and P.D. Strevens, *The Linguistic Sciences and Language Teaching*. London, Longman, 1964.

Holdcroft, D., Meaning and illocutionary acts. In Parkinson (ed.) 1968.

Hornby, A.S., Vocabulary control — history and principles. ELT 8/1 1953.

Hymes, D., The ethnography of speaking. In J.A. Fishman (ed.) *Readings in the Sociology of Language*. The Hague, Mouton, 1968.

Institut Pédagogique National, *Le Français Fondamental*. (1er degré), Paris.

Jespersen, O., *The Philosophy of Grammar*. London, Allen and Unwin, 1924.

Labov, W., *The Study of Non-standard English*. National Council of Teachers of English (U.S.A.), 1969.

Lado, R., *Language Teaching*. New York, McGraw-Hill, 1964.

Lee, W.R., Grading. ELT 17/3, 17/4, 18/2, 1962/63.

Littlewood W.T., Role-performance and language teaching. IRAL 13/3, 1975.

Lyons, J., *Introduction to Theoretical Linguistics*. Cambridge, Cambridge University Press, 1968.

Mackey, W.F., *Language Teaching Analysis*. London, Longman, 1965.

Mackey, W.F. and J.-G. Savard, The indices of coverage: a new dimension in lexicometrics. IRAL 5/2 & 3, 1967.

Michéa, R., Mots fréquents et mots disponibles. Les Langues Modernes, 47.

Parkinson, G.H.R. (ed.), *The Theory of Meaning*. London, Oxford University Press, 1968.

Peck, A.J., Talking to some purpose. In G.E. Perren and J.L.M. Trim (eds.), *Applications of Linguistics*. Cambridge, Cambridge University Press, 1971.

Reibel, D.A., Language learning analysis. IRAL 7/4, 1969.

Richards, I.A., *Basic English and its Uses*. London, Kegan Paul, 1943.

Richards, J.C., A psycholinguistic measure of vocabulary selection. IRAL 8/2, 1970.

Roget, P.M., *Thesaurus of English Words and Phrases*. Revised, modernized and abridged by R.A. Dutch. London, Penguin, 1966.

Searle, J.R., *Speech Acts*. Cambridge, Cambridge University Press, 1970.

Weinreich, U., On the semantic structure of language. In J.H. Greenberg (ed.), *Universals of Language*. Cambridge, M.I.T. Press, 2nd ed. 1966.

Widdowson, H.G., The teaching of rhetoric to students of science and technology. In *Science and Technology in a Second Language*. London, Centre for Information on Language Teaching and Research, 1971.

Wilkins, D.A., The linguistic and situational content of the common core in a unit/credit system. In *Systems Development in Adult Language Learning*. Strasbourg, Council of Europe, 1973.

Wilkins, D.A., Grammatical, situational and notional syllabuses. In A. Verdoodt (ed.), *Proceedings of the Third International Congress of Applied Linguistics*, Volume 2. Heidelberg, Julius Groos, 1974.

Wilkins, D.A., Notional syllabuses and the concept of a minimum adequate grammar. In Corder, S.P. and E. Roulet (eds.), *Linguistic Insights in Applied Linguistics*. Brussels, AIMAV, Paris, Didier, 1974.

INDEX OF NOTIONAL CATEGORIES

This index relates to the major and minor categories proposed for the notional framework. Reference is made both to the inventory of categories in Chapter Two and to any other occurrences in the text. Items are indexed in the form in which they are listed in Chapter Two (i.e. in general as a verb or noun). Grammatical categories are given in the General Index.

GENERAL INDEX